Praise for
Now and Not Yet

"In a culture that has grown unkind to marriage and the marriage-minded, Jennifer Marshall's analysis of the facts we live with and the faith that sustains us offers guidance and hope for young women. You may be single, but you do not have to be alone. Jennifer Marshall shows the way."

—WILLIAM J. BENNETT, Washington Fellow–The Claremont Institute, and host of *Bill Bennett's Morning in America*

"Jennifer Marshall rescues the dreary notion of 'contentment' from passive resignation and recharges it with a robust faith in God that results in vigorous, purposeful living.... Singles and nonsingles alike will find this brand of contented living liberating, energizing, and fulfilling."

—CAROLYN CUSTIS JAMES, author of *When Life and Beliefs Collide* and *Lost Women of the Bible*

"If we value marriage, we should value and mentor those among us who want to get there but are not there yet. In *Now and Not Yet,* her faith-and-research-based book, Jennifer Marshall not only brings to light this un-addressed reality of modern life, but gives her fellow single traditional women the pep talk they need. Post-twenties singleness can be a lonely time for the marriage-minded; Jennifer Marshall has made it less so."

—KATHRYN JEAN LOPEZ, editor of *National Review Online*

"Jennifer Marshall has a fresh, positive, God-centered perspective on singleness as one of the many callings we live by in the Christian life. *Now and Not Yet* is about much more than marital status; it's about loving and serving Jesus in the space between the way things are and the way we expect them to be. Marshall is honest about life's struggles and open to the legitimate desire to be married during what she calls 'the unexpected in-between.' What she writes is full of biblical and practical wisdom for pursuing single-minded devotion to God and finding joyful contentment in His unique plan for your life."

—PHILIP GRAHAM RYKEN, author of *The Message of Salvation* and *Ryken's Bible Handbook,* and senior minister of Tenth Presbyterian Church in Philadelphia, Pennsylvania

"With sensitivity and a sharp-edged knowledge of God's Word, Jennifer Marshall reveals the sweet and satisfying answer to our deepest longings, helping us all—whether married or single—find true pleasure in God. Thank you, Jennifer, for shining so much light on an oft-troubling topic."

—JONI EARECKSON TADA, JAF International Disability Center

"In her insightful and hopeful meditation on contemporary singlehood, Jennifer Marshall breaks through the tired stereotypes of the single woman as desperate for marriage or obsessed with career. She makes the compelling case that 'Christian, single, and content' is not an oxymoron but another pathway for women to fulfill God's calling for their lives. This book is essential reading not only for single women of all ages but for their mothers, fathers, friends, and faith communities."

—BARBARA DAFOE WHITEHEAD, author of *The Divorce Culture: Rethinking Our Commitment to Marriage and Family* and *Why There Are No Good Men Left: The Romantic Plight of the New Single Woman,* and codirector of the National Marriage Project, Rutgers

now and
not yet

To Ellen,

With blessings

for the journey.

Jennifer Marshall

11·07·07

now and not yet

not yet

Making Sense of Single Life
in the Twenty-First Century

JENNIFER A. MARSHALL

MULTNOMAH
BOOKS

Now and Not Yet
Published by Multnomah Books
12265 Oracle Boulevard, Suite 200
Colorado Springs, CO 80921
A division of Random House Inc.

Citations for quoted and referenced material are included in the notes section at the
end of the book.

Details in some anecdotes and stories have been changed to protect the identities of
the persons involved.

ISBN 978-1-59052-649-1

Published in association with The Livingstone Corporation
(www.LivingstoneCorp.com).

Library of Congress Cataloging-in-Publication Data
Marshall, Jennifer A.
    Now and not yet / Jennifer A. Marshall. — 1st ed.
        p. cm.
    Includes bibliographical references.
    ISBN 978-1-59052-649-1
    1. Single women—Religious life. I. Title.
BV4596.S5M3 2007
248.8'432—dc22

                                    2007001659

Printed in the United States of America
2007—First Edition

10 9 8 7 6 5 4 3 2 1 0

With gratitude for my family,
by birth and by grace.

Contents

Introduction: The Big Question 1

Part 1: The Unexpected Now

1   Off the Map 13

2   Life in the Unexpected In-Between 24

Part 2: Betwixt and Between: Betting on Marriage and Biding Time

3   Equal Opportunity Confusion 39

4   Mistaken for a Career Woman 54

Part 3: Then and Now: What's Become of Romance?

5   Closed Roads and Old Scripts 71

6   Bartering at the Have-It-All Bazaar 84

7   Working at Romance 93

Part 4: A Call from Now to Not Yet

8   The Sense of Callings 103

9   Called to Contentment: Living Happily,
    Here and Now 111

10 Callings as Catalyst and Compass 118

11   How Will I Know? Making Sense of Choices
        in Single Life 126

Part 5: Living Right Now

12   Mirroring the Image of God 143
13   Choosing Community 155
14   Honorable Intentions 160
15   Marking Progress 167

Epilogue: Corporate Responsibility: Notes to Parents,
        Church Leaders, and the Public-Policy Community ... 173
Notes 185
Acknowledgments 197

The Big Question

Fall has settled on Nashville, where I've dropped in for a weekend stay at the home of married friends who have two little girls. On Saturday afternoon we head for a puppet show at the downtown library. Maggie is six months pregnant with number three, so we tell her to take the front seat of the car. Thomas is driving, and I'm sandwiched between the two girls in their car seats in the back of the Ford Explorer.

One side effect of the pregnancy is that the girls' chatter often revolves around babies. As we drive across a wide intersection, four-year-old Mary Pierson asks me, "Do you have a baby?"

"No."

"Why not?"

"Because I'm not married," I explain.

"Why aren't you married?"

Hmm. Children have a knack for posing theological stumpers. As if we single women wouldn't like to have God answer that question ourselves.

From Baby Dolls
to Marriage

The next morning the girls ask me to read them some stories. I can tell they're in the mood for a fairy tale. They've got Snow White fig-urines in hand and offer me the choice of two books that both end with varia-tions on the theme of girl marrying boy and living hap-pily ever after.

Later that day, their daddy turns the questions on his daughter: "Mary Pierson, do you want to get married?"

"Yes."

"Why do you want to get married?"

"Because I want to be a mommy!"

Little girls learn early to love marriage and family.

Yet the trend of the last generation is that more young women are spending more years single—and many would say that's not by choice. The average age of first marriage has climbed more than four years since our parents' generation.

Not surprisingly, the circumstances of singleness can some-times be perplexing. Few of us received specific guidance about this particular phase of life as we were growing up. Frankly, no one seems to have expected it. Nor, with few exceptions, has there been much investigation of the disconnect between our expectations and reality—either how this gap came to be or how we as indi-vidual women should deal with the divide now that we're in the midst of it.

A Life Full of Callings

Thomas and Maggie are right to raise their daughters to desire marriage and children, just as it's appropriate for us as adult single women to maintain our own hope for those things.

The challenge for us singles, then, is to keep that desire in perspective. The most important questions are not, *Why am I not married? When will I get married?* or, *Whom will I marry?* Rather, they are, *How am I supposed to be content today while hoping for something more? What's my purpose here and now?* and, *Do I trust God in this unexpected in-between?* Answering these questions is the key to making sense of singleness.

The challenge is to live in the present purposefully and to lead a contented life even while particular desires remain unfulfilled. That kind of contentment depends on a sense of purpose outside our own feelings. It rests in the conviction that there is a grand design to our lives, and that the design has an Author. Our knowledge of that design may be incomplete, but its Author has made Himself known to us, and that helps us perceive how He works in our lives and in the world around us.

When God calls us to Himself, it transforms the purposes for which we live. To respond to that call is to view relationships, responsibilities, gifts, and opportunities as His purposes in our lives. These purposes are our *callings*—the things we are equipped by God to do in our individual situations throughout all the seasons of our lives. This perspective on life as a set of callings from God helps a woman get her bearings when singleness gets confusing—anchoring her identity, giving her a sense of belonging, setting a direction for her life's activities, and shaping her overall sense of purpose.

Because there are many ways in which each of us lives out our first call to God throughout the changing circumstances of a lifetime, this book uses the term *callings* to refer to those individual means through which we are to follow Him in our own situations.

The plural *callings* is meant to distinguish these from the singular purpose of that first call to Him. It is also intended to help us avoid the trap of elevating any one purpose here on earth—other than the pursuit of God—to the place where we confuse it for our whole life purpose. God's multiple callings in each of our lives may include marriage, but that is not the full story of His grand design for any of us. Being too focused on marriage (or its absence) may lead to neglect of our other callings at hand or cause us to miss the fulfillment He intends for us in each of those callings. Glorifying God should be the organizing principle of life. Marriage is only a means to that end, not to be confused for the end itself. Singleness is a part of God's design for life now, one aspect of a full—and complete—life.

Attaining contentment doesn't require us to suppress the desire for marriage, but it does mean we have to keep it in proper perspective. When desire grows into preoccupation, it edges out contentment and causes us to doubt God's faithfulness and goodness. When desire becomes a sense of entitlement—that God owes us what we want—it deprives us of gratitude for what He is doing outside our expectations.

Life is about more than marital status, and singleness is more than a holding pattern. This book is about redeeming the time between the now and the not yet for which we hope.

Where Now?

The chapters ahead address some of the major spiritual and practical struggles that single women commonly face today, and the context in which they meet them. Part 1, "The Unexpected Now," describes the wrestling that goes on in the hearts and minds of many single women as they confront unmet expectations about marriage and family, some of which are inspired by life patterns of the past that are becoming less common today.

Parts 2 and 3—"Betwixt and Between: Betting on Marriage and Biding Time" and "Then and Now: What's Become of Romance?"—discuss cultural changes since our mothers' generation. These have left women with many choices about their future, yet it seems more difficult to meet and marry a suitable match. What's more, in this new context a professionally successful single woman may discover that others assume she's more interested in a career than marriage. For the women described in this book, however, singleness is a fact of life more than a choice of lifestyle. They haven't been avoiding marriage; they're more likely feeling confused that marriage has avoided them.

Looking back at the well-charted course to marriage of generations past, extended singleness today can feel rather rudderless. We may have expected some sort of autopilot to carry us smoothly to

Destination Marriage. Instead, life between college and marriage can seem more like killing time than making personal progress. At times, the weight of cultural assumptions, concern about others' perceptions or misperceptions, and the force of our own feelings about singleness can build up like a perfect storm, leaving us disoriented about where we should be heading in life right now. Either set of conditions—the doldrums or the near drowning—can cloud our thinking about choices, such as whether to get another degree or to buy a house. Part 4, "A Call from Now to Not Yet," explains how God's callings can help clear away some of that confusion by providing a navigational system for life. Part 5, "Living Right Now," offers specific suggestions on establishing solid footing for the journey through singleness.

Putting a Face on It

Each section of this book opens with a story that shows how individual women have cleared away personal and cultural confusion to make sense of their lives before God. Part 1 begins with Hilary, who in her late twenties pursues an opportunity that leads her off the beaten path to Iraq. Although few of us go anywhere so dangerous or far from home, many young women experience feelings similar to Hilary's when God prompts them to use their gifts in new and challenging situations.

In part 2, Emma and Carli, both wrestling with academic and professional decisions, like many young women, wonder how far to pursue higher education when their desire is to marry and have children. Is it a waste of time and money to go to law school or medical school? Although they made very different decisions, both women have a sense of contentment that they are where God wants them to be.

In part 3, a snapshot of three single thirtysomethings (two friends and me) is juxtaposed with the experiences of our parents' generation. Although our paths have taken turns we did not expect, God still works in circumstances that weren't "supposed" to happen.

Who Says?

In preparing to write this book, I asked a number of single women about their outlook on singleness and experiences during this season of life. These interviews focused on the segment of the American population whose life experience is the subject of this book: never-married Christian women in their midtwenties to midforties who are generally well-educated and living mostly in suburban or urban areas. Their experiences and expressions give real-life context to the themes addressed in this book. In many cases, names of those quoted or referenced have been changed.

I conducted in-depth interviews with twelve women in four cities, and another three women provided extensive written feedback to a questionnaire. Thirty-one women ranging in age from late twenties to midforties participated in focus groups in Washington DC, New York City, Chicago, and Long Beach, California. None of the forty-six women in the interviews or focus groups has married; all are professing Christians; many have earned advanced degrees.

To elicit a broad response, I conducted an online survey to

which 650 unmarried women over the age of twenty responded. Almost all had never married, though a few had previously been married. Respondents were split almost evenly between urban and suburban areas across the United States, with less than ten percent from rural areas. A large majority are Christians, and eight out of ten attend church or other religious services regularly. Nearly all have graduated from college, and more than a quarter have master's degrees. Half have plans to pursue further education.

With few exceptions, these women want to get married. As teenagers, more than half thought they would be married by the age of twenty-five. Some of the younger respondents still could marry before their ideal wedding date, but many—perhaps most—will not.

While this book addresses some of the issues that are specific to the lives of single women, I sought some male perspective on these matters as well. I gathered input through focus groups, interviews, and a questionnaire from thirteen unmarried Christian men between the ages of twenty-three and forty-four.

As increasing numbers of women and men spend more of their lives unmarried, the topic of singleness demands greater theological and sociological attention. A complex set of cultural and economic factors has contributed to the trend of marrying later and to the disappearance of well-marked routes that once led clearly to marriage.

On a sociological level, one could question whether later marriage is a good thing for individuals or for society as a whole, and one could argue for more community support of singles seeking to form relationships leading to marriage. But these issues are described briefly only to set the stage on which individual lives play out.

This book touches on the cultural changes to show that a sense of confusion about the difficulty of entering marriage is not merely an interior and personal struggle, but is one in which constantly changing social dynamics play a significant part. These dynamics require corporate attention, but reckoning with them individually can help a single woman sort out her experience and sharpen her perspective.

Plenty of questions could be raised about why we're still single. But a more important and more immediate concern is our personal responsibility for our lives and general outlook. Getting that in order is key to other things as well. "Contentment is attractive in a woman," as one single man put it.

The central focus of this book is the part of the puzzle that we as single women are responsible for: tending to the spiritual and practical aspects of our own day-to-day lives. Single young women must live in the world as it meets them today, and many are simply trying to figure out how to seek contentment now as well as pursue dreams not yet realized. This book is by, about, and for women who find themselves in that unexpected place.

PART 1

The Unexpected Now

One

Off the Map

No one was there to meet Hilary when she stepped off the plane. Not that she had expected anyone, but it was another reminder of isolation in her sense of purpose. Here she was, a blond, blue-eyed, twenty-eight-year-old civilian heading to a new job in the midst of a military occupation in the Middle East.

Alone and unable to hide the fact that she was an American, she had to look like she'd done this before. She needed to get to her hotel without being ripped off—or worse. She managed to trade dollars for dinar, but she knew her ignorance would show as soon as she asked about the price of a cab ride. So she questioned one driver, then used that information to barter with a second.

Forty-five minutes later, she arrived at her hotel.

The next morning she boarded a military aircraft to fly from Kuwait to Baghdad. Strapped into a jump seat with her back against the inner wall of the airplane, she fell asleep and woke up with the muzzle of a gun leaning against her—her soldier seatmate had fallen asleep too.

But no one sleeps through the drama of a Baghdad landing. The plane dove and rolled from side to side, maneuvering wildly to avoid any unfriendly fire. It gave her the sickening sensation that her life was now completely out of her control.

The road from Baghdad International Airport to the U.S. military–secured Green Zone in the city became a notoriously dangerous passage. But that day in July she made the trek in an unarmored thin-skin vehicle—and her driver was nonchalant about whether the passengers should wear the body armor they had been issued. That was when she realized she couldn't make any assumptions that others would look out for her security. She wasted no time in heaving on her bulletproof vest packed with heavy armor plates.

Out of the Green Zone

Baghdad's Republican Palace, once the seat of Saddam Hussein's regime, was now the headquarters of the Coalition Provisional Authority (CPA) and the hub of activities in the Green Zone. An air force colonel met her there.

"Miss White, welcome to Baghdad. You're going to spend the night here and go to Hillah in the morning."

Apparently there was some confusion. Hillah was not a part of her plans. Going to a remote city somewhere to the south did *not* sound appealing.

But the colonel was insistent.

Hilary resolved to accept the change for the time being, go to

Hillah, and get herself back to the Green Zone as soon as possible. She wanted to leave most of her belongings in Baghdad as collateral, but the colonel informed her everything would be going with her. The next morning they packed up her three massive black trunks— filled with six months' worth of clothes, food, and supplies—and left for Hillah.

They rolled through arid desert for an hour and a half on a highway Saddam Hussein had built for his military. An oasis of date palm trees emerged in the midst of the desert dust as they neared Hillah. As they crossed over a bridge that spanned a tributary of the Euphrates near the ruins of Babylon, Hilary thought, *This is where it all began.* It was like stepping back into ancient history.

There was no exit from the highway to the road that led to their destination on the outskirts of Hillah. So they made their own, off-roading over uneven terrain before intersecting a route that ran to the U.S. compound.

The residence where Hilary and others stayed was a hotel, parts of which Saddam's Baathist regime had used as a brothel. Almost every Iraqi Hilary met had lost family members to the violence of Saddam's regime.

But things were changing in Hillah. Widows on the edge of destitution were learning how to make a living. Schools were being repaired, and student texts from the prior regime were being replaced. Iraqi Shia started painting their houses vibrant colors to celebrate their newfound freedom. Hillah was an oasis of good news, and Hilary had come to Iraq to share the country's good news with the rest of the world. There was no better place for her to be. God's sleight of hand had moved her beyond her own stubborn expectations for a purpose that would leave her more content than if she'd had it her way.

How Did I Get Here?

Hilary never dreamed she'd be going to Iraq when she neared age thirty; she thought she'd have been married with children by this time.

Lots of other unmarried twenty- and thirtysomething women expected to be married by this age too, but instead they find themselves in the midst of adventures they never imagined. Marriage is not as prompt a suitor as it was in our mothers' generation. Back when those of us in our midthirties were born, the average age of first marriage for women was just under twenty-one. Today it is over twenty-five.

Whether by nature or nurture or a combination of forces, little girls usually grow up wanting to be wives and mothers, not going to work in a war zone. Nine out of ten high-school senior girls say that a good marriage and family life are important for their future—and *that* statistic hasn't changed much in twenty-five years, in spite of the hike in marriage age.

Our culture in general, and the Christian subculture in particular, fosters in young women a desire for marriage and the presumption that marriage will be a part of life sooner rather than later.

Each of us has her own script for the perfect life, spliced together from scraps of happy-ending movies and sentimental stories. But almost invariably in these fictional scenarios, marriage makes its entrance by age twenty-five, thirty at the latest.

Reality, however, regularly departs from the script. Almost six out of ten women today are not married by age twenty-five. Three out of ten are not married by age thirty.

As unmarried women, we may instead find ourselves in situations that, while not as intense as Hilary's, leave us out of our element, occasionally confused, and every so often with a pit-in-the-stomach realization that life is not tidily within our control. Even when we are confident of our callings—knowing that we are in the right place doing the right thing for the moment—we can experience fear, insecurity, and uncertainty about all kinds of practical details in life. We struggle with our own and others' conceptions of singleness, especially when we're surrounded by so much cultural confusion about male-female relations, women's roles, and personal fulfillment.

For many of us in the midst of this confusion, however, being single is no more—and no less—of a statement than, *This is what God has for me now.*

Finding the Way

Hilary knew that she was meant to be in Iraq. But her sense of purpose was under assault the minute she set foot alone in the Middle East.

Months before, she had gotten the idea that she'd like to help in the rebuilding of Iraq. Then she waited for weeks to hear whether a public relations post would open up for her. Waiting to go to Iraq was filled with uncertainty, just as following other promptings from God often are; one day an opening would appear, and the next day it would close. All she could do was watch for a door to begin to open, first just a crack, then partway. When it finally opened fully, she could walk through. Many doors had to open, however, before she got to Iraq.

"You never know for sure you're going to Iraq until you're on the plane and it's taking off," she tells others who think they're headed that way. One day she was getting vaccinated at the Pentagon, and a few days later she went to pick up her bulletproof vest. Soon after, she was on an airplane to the Middle East. "And it wasn't until I was flying across the Atlantic that I had the *Aha!* moment—that satisfaction when hope finally becomes reality."

After *Aha!*

When Hilary closed the door to her room that first night in Hillah, she was totally overwhelmed. She had never run a public affairs office, let alone one in a war zone. But self-doubt and second guesses were edged out a few days later when she learned she'd be traveling to Ramadi for an Iraqi town hall meeting. There was nothing to do but get ready for work.

Her first challenge was to figure out what to wear. Being choosy that morning had nothing to do with mood; it was all about conforming to a foreign dress code, and she had to seek advice about it from American men she hardly knew. The khakis she put on left her ankles showing, so she pulled on socks. She wore a shirt with three-quarter-length sleeves and buttoned it all the way up, even though it was well over a hundred degrees. As for a head covering, she didn't know what would be expected, so she stuffed a scarf in her bag.

Nothing was straightforward. Even issuing a press release on the progress in Ramadi was complicated. It meant scrambling to find an Arabic interpreter and an Arabic keyboard, then figuring out how to get it to the proper press outlets. The learning curve was steep.

There is a right time for everything, she determined. A time to ask questions, a time not to ask questions; a time to act like you know what you're doing, a time to admit you have no idea. And as one of very few women among some two hundred men in the compound, it was always the time to be strong and clear about where she stood with them—but to be feminine all the same. "A girl should never go out without her gun, her flak jacket, and her lipstick," was her rule of thumb.

The duties of many of the civilians on the compound included assisting with security, so Hilary jumped in. She decided she wanted to keep a weapon with her, and a marine heading home left her his 9 mm Beretta.

"Ma'am, do you know what you're doing?" some soldiers would ask when they saw her carrying a weapon.

"I'm from Texas," she'd explain, and they would smile and leave her alone.

Her military colleagues taught her how to guard her quadrant in the vehicle convoys and how to read the crowd of onlookers for trouble as they traveled. She was always on the lookout. "That's when I learned I had to think like a terrorist might think."

It would be a bad day, she knew, if there was an attack and she had to use the gun. But it would be a worse day if she didn't have the gun to use.

Alone in the Unexpected

One of her American colleagues started a women's center in Hillah. Many of the Iraqi women had lost husbands, fathers, and brothers in the Iran-Iraq war that had dominated their lives in the 1980s. Other male family members simply disappeared or were murdered by Saddam's henchmen. In Iraq, when the breadwinner dies, his widow goes to live with his relatives. When so many men in that family are gone, the women are left to provide for themselves and their children. In south central Iraq around Hillah, women made up a majority of the population. At the women's center, these women could learn to sew clothes or to use a computer.

Women didn't come to the center to abandon the veil or flout their religious traditions. They came trying to make their way through a chapter of life far different from what they had expected.

For all the sadness and loss they had suffered, the Iraqi women were industrious and hopeful. They loved their new opportunities. "There were so many good stories coming out of the women's center and out of Hillah," Hilary recalled.

Security in the Shadow

It wasn't all happy endings, however. There was bad news too, like the ambush and massacre of a roommate and two colleagues, and the deaths of fellow Americans and new Iraqi friends.

There were times when the sense of insecurity was overwhelming. In one of those despairing moments, Hilary turned to a member of the security detail—a big, tough guy—and asked him if he ever got scared. Yes, he said, he did. And then he started to recite Psalm 91:

> He who dwells in the shelter of the Most High
>> will rest in the shadow of the Almighty.
> I will say of the LORD, "He is my refuge and my fortress,
>> my God, in whom I trust."

> Surely he will save you from the fowler's snare
>> and from the deadly pestilence.
> He will cover you with his feathers,
>> and under his wings you will find refuge;
>> his faithfulness will be your shield and rampart.
> You will not fear the terror of night,
>> nor the arrow that flies by day,
> nor the pestilence that stalks in the darkness,
>> nor the plague that destroys at midday.
> A thousand may fall at your side,
>> ten thousand at your right hand,
>> but it will not come near you.

You will only observe with your eyes
>   and see the punishment of the wicked.

If you make the Most High your dwelling—
>   even the LORD, who is my refuge—
then no harm will befall you,
>   no disaster will come near your tent.
For he will command his angels concerning you
>   to guard you in all your ways;
they will lift you up in their hands,
>   so that you will not strike your foot against a stone.
You will tread upon the lion and the cobra;
>   you will trample the great lion and the serpent.

"Because he loves me," says the LORD, "I will rescue him;
>   I will protect him, for he acknowledges my name.
He will call upon me, and I will answer him;
>   I will be with him in trouble,
>   I will deliver him and honor him.
With long life will I satisfy him
>   and show him my salvation."

Hilary spent about a year in Iraq before returning to the United States. She's been back to Iraq three times since, and now she has a different outlook on the war zone. "I read Psalm 91 when we're getting close to landing in Iraq, and I share it with others who may have similar fears.

"Right now, it's harder for me to stay here than to go back. I've realized that I'm here to work on being content in this office life, and to learn more about walking with the Lord wherever I am.

"I know at some point I will have to stop going into the war zone. There will be a time when I will want to settle down and get married, and I won't be able to do this anymore. And that's fine."

Her unexpected adventure has stretched her idea of what the future might look like, however, and she adds a caveat: "But I would like to marry someone who knows the sound of a mortar going off."

Two

Life in the Unexpected In-Between

Blessed is the person whose heart is set on a pilgrimage, says one of the psalms. But many a single woman looks for the place where her heart can set up home. "Settling down" is a psychological comfort zone complete with husband, house, kids, car, and suburban lifestyle.

Many of us grew up thinking that would all come along as a matter of course. Those were the days of autopilot. Forward motion didn't require much thought or deliberation; third grade propelled one to fourth grade, fourth to fifth, and so on. Each fall brought new school clothes and lunchboxes, and every so often a new addition to the routine, like basketball or French or a new kid in class. Entering high school was a major milestone, but it only reset the clock for another four years.

After that it's fairly easy to coast through the next several years on autopilot. The course is well defined, and decisions come along on an established timetable: choose a college, choose a major, get a job (or go to grad school).

Many of us had the general impression that this perpetual forward motion would land us at Destination Marriage sometime in our midtwenties. Others pictured a more scenic route through some independence in their twenties and marriage by about age thirty. Either way, when reality deviates from the ideal course, the discrepancy between our experience and our expectations can be disorienting.

Sooner or later—and the sooner the better—the autopilot that propels us from adolescence to adulthood breaks down or runs out of gas. When it stops short of the desired destination, something else has to kick in if we're going to make progress toward the purposes for which we were created.

Beyond Autopilot

Where autopilot ends, the pilgrimage begins. Welcome to the wilderness—sometimes daunting, sometimes exhilarating, always challenging.

In this no man's land there are few well-worn paths. We're off-roading outside our own (and others') expectations of where life was supposed to take us. No one can tell us when or if we'll reach that elusive destination of marriage or what we'll encounter between here and there. Nothing we do seems to bring it any closer. A wedding date isn't a solo decision.

Like it or not, there is no MapQuest for life, no place we can go for preprinted directions that tell us, "Head east after college," or, "Slow down, watch for a man." The guide-to-life details just aren't that clear. As a result, we need to develop our own sharp sense of direction, alertness, and a balanced pace, and that takes some work.

On our own in this unexpected in-between, we are responsible for tending to our own security—physical, material, and spiritual. Life stretches us further than we would like or thought we could handle. We develop a stronger sense of self and learn self-reliance for things we might have preferred to have a man around to do. We can feel lost and get lonely, and then crave the companionship found in marriage all the more.

Most of the choices about which way to head aren't so much between right and wrong as between equally unclear routes. It all brings us back to one of life's most basic questions: what are we aiming for, anyway?

Meanwhile, the horizon is expanding. Unexpected circumstances test the talents we knew we had, and the need for improvisation makes us recognize other gifts we'd never noticed before.

We discover empathy for others in their own unexpected detours and find out that God's work doesn't have us all on the same route. We learn to discern God's guidance and develop a compass for life. We grow in understanding of what it means to walk with God.

And we walk in hope of reaching the next gracious plateau, from which we can look back and see the purpose in this part of life's meandering path.

Whose Map Is It, Anyhow?

The dissonance between the real and ideal became especially acute for me at age twenty-eight. Over the next five years, I moved five times, including across the Atlantic Ocean and back. In August 2000, I left for France to teach international students for a year. Picture the quintessential French town, and you've got a good image of Sainte-Foy-lès-Lyon, where I lived two flights above a bakery in a cream-colored stucco building near the center of town on a tiny street barely wide enough for a car to pass.

Our school was a ten-minute walk down a hill overlooking the peninsula between the Rhône and Saône rivers on which France's second city, Lyon, has grown up for more than twenty centuries. I taught the history of four of those centuries, from 1500 to 1900, to eleventh-grade students (little nomads themselves) from Norway, Australia, France, and the United States.

Like many first-year teachers, I learned more than my students did, particularly given the classroom that we had access to. When we wanted to study the French Revolution, we went to the government archives nearby and read about the siege of Lyon, when it resisted the revolutionary government. Sometimes after the school day had ended, I would go on walks past an early church built in memory of Christians martyred there in AD 177, or a Gallo-Roman amphitheater built around 15 BC.

At the end of the school year, I decided that I would return to the States—without a job, a place to live, or any clarity about my next step. Now, I come from a family famous for leaving major trip details like packing until the last minute (my uncle and his family have more than one story of nearly missing an international flight). True to form, I left too much for the last day and had to pull an all-nighter to get everything done before my trans-Atlantic flight the next morning. Sitting in the midst of half-packed boxes at 3 a.m., adrenaline gave way to angst.

I was leaving a place I'd never thought I would be to go to another situation that, as yet, had no form—a déjà vu from the previous year. The troubling fog that had followed me across the Atlantic showed no signs of clearing once I returned stateside. Everything was disconcertingly vague (though, frankly, *most* things look pretty bleak at 3 a.m.).

This was a phase of life I had never anticipated. Events had strayed so wide of the target that my dreams and expectations had little relevance to the current context. I wanted more information about where I was headed. I found myself asking, *Why? Where are we going, God?*

What makes us think we can demand concierge treatment from God, as though He needs to consult us about whether we'd prefer the direct or scenic route? God isn't running a tourist agency, and His road maps don't work like that. God's route often takes all kinds of inexplicable turns and leaves us asking those gut-gnawing questions like, *Are we there yet?*

After returning to the States, I began to notice that this impression of off-course existence wasn't unique to me. A number of friends and acquaintances seemed similarly mystified that their single life was lasting much longer than they had anticipated. Younger women, meanwhile, appeared unprepared for and unsettled by the prospect of lingering singleness.

Mind the Gap: Between Life Here and Life Hoped For

In the gap between our expectations and reality, discontentment tends to spring up like a weed. Three-fourths of the 650 survey respondents to my online survey described themselves as currently content, in general, but only one-half said they were content with their singleness. Fifteen percent said that singleness had caused them to doubt their faith. As teens, nine out of ten of these women pictured themselves married, and nearly as many say they still want to marry.

The gap between expectation and actual circumstance becomes the proving ground of faith. Living in the gap is an ongoing wrestling match with doubts and serious questions:

How well do I know God after all? Do I really trust Him?

How do I live in the present, deliberately, contentedly, and purposefully, while desiring something more for the future, something that is, in large part, out of my control? How do I continue to desire marriage without letting it consume me?

Can I trust my own judgment about life choices? Should I get a master's degree? Should I buy a place or rent? Will looking for ways to advance at work lessen my chances of marriage? What are legitimate criteria for making decisions?

Crocker Versus Friedan: When Neither Betty Will Do

A young woman, from birth to graduation, between reading fairy tales about Prince Charming and hearing that she can be *anything* she wants when she grows up—teacher, doctor, lawyer, astronaut, even president—receives a wide range of competing recruitment messages about what she should do with her life.

Some signals say she should develop her marketable talents, seize professional opportunities, and strive for career satisfaction. Other messages tell women that their highest purpose is to marry and have children. Confronted by these rival perspectives, a young woman may feel not only personally conflicted but also pushed like a pawn in the great cultural debate over whether women's worth should be measured by Betty Crocker or Betty Friedan.

Whatever other answers we may have given about what we wanted to be when we grew up, the fact is, for many of us the waiting period for marriage has been much longer than we would have liked or expected. In the meantime, necessity usually demands that we get on some sort of career track, whether we like it or not.

For the single woman who enjoys her work but also anticipates marriage, the debate over whether to measure a woman's worth by mother value or market value doesn't really connect with life as she currently knows it. On the mother scale she doesn't rank at all, but she hopes to one day. On the market scale she may score high, but she doesn't want that to count against her prospects for achieving the traditional goals of marriage and motherhood.

SHE SAYS: IMAGINING A DECADE
OF SINGLENESS AHEAD

"Girls feel unfulfilled, unworthy, missing out, because they're not dating and not on the marriage track and don't see it on the horizon," said Sharon, twenty-nine, who works with university women. "Two of the senior girls are getting married this summer, and the others look at them as if to say, *They're more together, they're on a better road, their life is better than mine.*"

I asked young women to picture themselves single ten years from now. Here are some of their responses:

Wow. I have never considered that. Thinking of that situation I feel sad and lonely.
—Erin, 25

I will have a lovely little apartment and take dancing lessons... Thinking about that is a feeling of rather intense contentment.
—Laura, 25

I would be extremely sad, even slightly depressed, and very disappointed. I would lack confidence in myself and doubt myself as being someone who is capable of finding love and being loved.
—Kate, 24

(continues on the next page)

It brings a feeling of pain and loneliness. Most of my friends are married with families, so I often feel like I'm being left behind. I feel alone.

—Anna, 26

I am not as concerned with being single as I am with the observation of others: "Why is she thirty-three and still single? What is wrong with her? Who can I set her up with?" The idea of being single for the next ten years does not scare me, but the stigma of being a single thirty-three-year-old sort of does.

—Gina, 23

I have friends at that point, and I often feel sad for them, but I don't think that they feel as sad as I do about it. Today I see that as sad, but at that point I would hope I would have good examples to show me how to honor God through that singleness. However, I very much desire to be married before then.

—Rachel, 25

My initial reaction is just to block this idea out. I know that's not a good reaction, so I begin to think through being single at forty, and I remind myself that God is the One who has numbered my days. He has promised to never leave me or forsake me, and I can trust in His faithful plan for my life.

—Kristin, 25

Ugh! I really hope that's not the case, but if it is, I hope I will have faith enough to know that God holds my every day and path in His hands—and His plan is perfect and will bring me more joy than anything I could come up with myself.

    —Ellen, 26

Loneliness, stemming from the fear that I will not have someone to share life with—both the joys and the trials.

    —Stephanie, 22

I feel a little discouraged, but only because I would like for my circumstances to be different ten years from now, married or single. I would like to be more independent, living on my own, etc. I guess it's hard to imagine not being married by then... After all, there's always eHarmony...just kidding... sort of!

    —Becky, 24

In one sense, I would be disappointed, because I do want to be married. Yet in another sense, I guess it would just depend on what I'm doing instead. If it was something that I loved, then it would be okay. I would need the balance of social interactions.

    —Paige, 23

Disappointment and dread.

    —Elizabeth, 27

What's more, neither perspective offers solid criteria for making sound decisions about the very practical concerns of her life between college and marriage.

From Twilight Zone to True North

Stranded between the autopilot of adolescence and the anchor of marriage, a girl can feel adrift in some twilight zone between legitimate episodes of her life. That's the risk of fixing our sights on Destination Marriage as the North Star. Rather than navigating surely, we're more likely to be chasing shooting stars and getting more and more disoriented in the process.

By contrast, God's call helps us orient ourselves toward a fixed point of reference: Himself. Not ourselves, not men, and not marriage. From there we can make sense of practical choices about jobs, continuing education, housing, and finances without getting confused by the bombardment of cultural assumptions, others' opinions, or our own feelings.

Choice has come to be regarded as the essential element of the modern American way of life: where we live, how we make a living, what we believe, what we do with our bodies. Choice is the essence of freedom, or so it goes.

But unlimited choice is not the same thing as unlimited freedom. Setting aside choices that are simply wrong or harmful in themselves, choosing from among good options is still a challenge. Too many choices—not to mention the voices of opinion about them—can be dizzying and disorienting. Choice, in and of itself, is not so liberating as the capacity to choose well. To choose well is to make a decision for the right reasons; *why* we choose something is as important as *what* we choose.

True freedom involves choosing that which allows us to direct our passions and energy toward the purposes for which we were created. The best guidance helps each one of us discern our own path within this maze of options, mapping it out with purpose rather than idling between milestones.

God's call provides that kind of guidance. A heart set on a pilgrimage is poised between what is and what God has yet to bring about after the next turn. It seeks purpose and joy in each part of that journey.

Balancing one's outlook between things here and things hoped for is a constant challenge. We can't control everything going on around us, but we are responsible for the disposition of our hearts toward those external circumstances. We're not responsible for what others might think of us and our decisions, but we are accountable for the choices we make.

The following sections of this book—parts 2 and 3—survey some of the cultural changes that have taken place over the last generation. These changes have resulted in new opportunities for women, but they also have brought with them new confusion. It leaves single women who'd like to be married in a tangle of social assumptions, perceptions, and personal expectations. Following God through that confusion is the challenge of walking by faith in new cultural territory.

PART 2

Betwixt and Between: Betting on Marriage and Biding Time

Three

Equal Opportunity Confusion

Emma grudgingly took the MCAT exam for medical school a second time, but the result was the same. She got only one acceptance letter, from the Uniformed Services medical school in Bethesda, Maryland. It was the town where she had grown up—at that point, not a mark in its favor.

Emma's father had told her he would pay for her undergraduate education at the University of Maryland only if she majored in biology and set her sights on med school. She would have preferred communications or French, but she went along with his plan. Biology turned out to be a good fit, but the prospect of medical school wasn't—especially when her only option seemed like such a stretch.

The Uniformed Services University of the Health Sciences trains doctors for careers in the military or the public health sector. Its major perk is that it is tuition-free, but the payback is ten years of service after graduation. For Emma, the decision was enormously daunting. Her father couldn't see what was holding her back. She agonized over it, and eventually she decided not to go.

Tension between Emma and her parents had been mounting for a number of years as her parents pushed her to perform academically. Now she was on her own without her parents' support.

When Emma left home, she headed for Philadelphia, where she knew of a community that would meet her with grace. She had spent summers there with a medical campus ministry. She completed her bachelor's and master's degrees in nursing at Penn. She bought a house and seriously dated a music artist.

Today, ten years after finishing undergraduate school, Emma is back in Maryland pursuing a PhD. She has reconciled with her father, who is now seventy-six and has been diagnosed with a chronic form of leukemia. With the country at war, her father has told her he never would have forgiven himself if she had gone to med school and been sent to Iraq and something had happened to her.

Emma had thought of the war scenario—and many others—when she played out the whole fourteen-year commitment in her mind. The major factor that didn't fit in that picture was getting married and having a family, something she dearly wanted. Not getting married was one of her worst fears at the time, and she figured medical school would be a turnoff to men.

Her parents had always wanted her to get married as well, but they had their own opinions about what would deter men—in particular, sports. Since the days of neighborhood kickball with her big brother, Emma had always liked sports. Her best friend, Kerri, convinced her to play soccer. "Try it, Emma. You'll like it," Kerri told her. So in eighth grade, Emma went out for the team and loved it. But her parents discouraged her from playing. "If you play soccer, your thighs will get big and then boys won't like you," her father told her. It was the kind of comment an adolescent girl doesn't forget.

Her mother thought she should play piano so she would stand out among women. At the age of eight, that wasn't much of an encouragement to keep playing, but she stuck with it through junior high.

The right appearance and demeanor were essential to attracting men and getting married, her mother advised her. Make a good first impression, be the life of the party, but make sure not to laugh too raucously. During high school and college, Emma got into the habit of playing that part.

Emma herself wondered if doing too well in school was a liability. Along the way, she'd often play down her intellect because it seemed to intimidate guys.

Too smart? Too athletic? Not animated enough? For Emma and others, the questions can pile up and leave a young woman wondering how to be herself and still attract a man. Sometimes it can seem like an either/or choice.

Education Versus Marriage?

For Carli, the question was whether or not to attend law school. "I struggled with the decision because of the expectation that Christian women should marry soon after graduation and begin raising a family. My desire to go to law school seemed out of sync with that. I did want to marry, and I was afraid that going to law school would mean I never would."

Then she talked to two women a few years older than she was, who had chosen not to go to law school because they each had thought they would get married and have a family. Neither had married, but each had met with professional success.

"Both encouraged me to go if I wanted to, and to trust God to bring along marriage in His timing, if it was His will. It was great advice. As I finished law school, I remember asking several people for advice on how to commit completely to my work while still remaining completely open to the possibility of marriage. I had few role models of single Christian women working with excellence in their careers, and few people really had any advice for me on that. I decided to head fully toward my work goals while I was single and to trust God's will and timing on marriage. I think it is a large part of why I have been so content being single."

While Carli was an intern just before law school, a friend who saw her résumé was surprised by her high grade point average and announced it to the other interns. Later, another friend said she had really shocked everyone by getting into a top law school. Apparently, it seemed out of keeping with her warm personality. "This puzzled me," said Carli, "as if there were a contradiction between being nice and being smart.

"In law school, a lot of my female classmates seemed hard or abrasive, at least at first. It seemed like they anticipated discrimination or felt like they had to prove they were smart and capable. This surprised me too.

"During finals, a friend and I put little gifts in our classmates' mailboxes to help alleviate stress (for them and for us). A male friend in the class made the comment, 'Why are you here? You're too nice for law school. You should be in elementary ed.'"

Carli had, in fact, majored in elementary education as an undergrad, but she didn't think changing vocational directions called for a personality change. "I saw no reason why I shouldn't be my happy self while pursuing academic and professional success. I'd rather be who I really am, so I made a conscious decision at that point to keep being who I am and to ignore the misperceptions people might have of me as a result."

The Accumulation of Assumptions

Even when our own spirits are at peace with God's purposes, that doesn't mean everyone else is.

Three years ago, Carli moved to the Bible Belt. "When I meet other Christian women, frequently the first question they ask me is if I'm married. Then they often ask me if I am engaged, and then if I am dating anyone.

"It never occurred to me that I would receive these kinds of responses from others as I followed God to where I believed He was calling me. I believe God has called us to live our lives to the fullest— developing the gifts and talents He has given us through the opportunities He has provided—whether we are single or married."

For Carli, that has meant taking a job as a pre-law professor at a Midwestern college. "I have experienced equal opportunities for men and women in some very tough educational and professional fields. More than that, I have seen women regularly rise to the top.

But what I'd like to see is not a focus on the equality of women, but a focus on the development of individual gifts and talents—whether we are male or female.

"My parents encouraged each of us kids (male or female) to pursue our dreams wholeheartedly. When I was about nine years old, I drew an elaborate architectural plan of my dream house. I wrote on the top, 'My dream house for when I get married one day.' I showed it to my mom, and she said, 'You don't have to wait to get married to build your dream house, honey. Build it whenever you want to.' That was such a revelation. It's been in the back of my mind ever since."

As for Emma, she has reconciled her own concepts of intellect, beauty, and spirit, thanks in part to a former boyfriend's influence. "He delighted in me as a whole person," she said. He encouraged her to pursue the PhD she's now completing. "Emma, this is a great opportunity," he told her. "You should go for it if you want to—but do you want to?"

"Hearing it framed that way was so freeing to me," she recalls. It didn't force her into a take-it-or-leave-it decision based upon someone else's opinion. She could size it up to see if it fit her abilities, her interests, who God had made her to be, and what He had made her to do.

Cultural assumptions, others' opinions, and personal preferences about what we should do with our lives have a way of accumulating like sediment on the original foundation. When all else is stripped away, we are accountable before God. Getting back to that bedrock requires making a way through layers of cultural confusion.

Taking stock of how feminism has complicated matters is a good place to start scratching the surface.

Good Daughters in an Age of Feminism

Unbeknown to most of us growing up in Generation X, the cultural scenery surrounding our childhood was changing dramatically. The changes have opened new opportunities, but have presented new challenges as well. Today, as adults, we find ourselves on routes where the intersections to marriage are not well marked, which makes it difficult to merge old dreams with new realities.

The shift began when feminist activists advancing their own social agenda also set about reshaping the landscape for girls. "The Girl Project" is what researcher Barbara Dafoe Whitehead calls it, marking its birth in 1972 with the signing of Title IX, the federal law that mandated gender equity in education. Though the law focused primarily on higher education, the principle could be applied to younger girls' activities as well, and feminists pursued a legal strategy that beat down the gates of Little League for girls to enter that and other fields in the years that followed. The Girl Project got eight New Jersey girls into Little League in 1974, and Shannon Faulkner into the Citadel in 1995.

Growing up in the midst of the Girl Project, those of us in Generation X (born between roughly 1963 and 1978), like Emma and Carli, experienced it mostly as a wider menu of extracurricular activities and academic opportunities. Girls' participation in high-school sports increased nearly 850 percent between 1971 and 2001. By the

1980s, it was no longer merely a feminist vanguard clamoring for girls' sports opportunities. Parents had jumped on the bandwagon, enthusiastically (if unknowingly) joining the cause as their daughters' first fans. The Girl Project "exploited two of the most powerful and unifying popular sentiments in American life—the love of sports and the love of the underdog competitor," says Whitehead.

In 1983, a made-for-television movie called *Quarterback Princess,* starring Helen Hunt, captured this agenda. *Quarterback Princess* was based loosely on the true story of Tami Maida, who just two years before became the first known quarterback also to be named homecoming queen.

In the movie, Tami convinces a wary coach, along with grudging spectators, that girls can play football too. She leads her Oregon high-school team to a state championship…then cleans up to be crowned homecoming queen.

Looking back at reviews, the movie is barely concealed Girl Project propaganda. I admit to being enamored of the plot as an eleven-year-old; it appealed to the natural tomboy streak so many of us had at that age. But it also had the appeal of a fairy-tale ending. It wouldn't have been nearly as attractive if quarterback Tami had left the locker room to spend the rest of homecoming night watching late-night television in the family room without a date.

Because It Was There

Very few girls would have been interested in breaking the gender barrier in varsity football or in the freshman class at a military academy.

Feminist ideology was the furthest thing from our minds when we were girls playing basketball at my Christian grade school.

Sure, we scoffed at our mothers' stories of the old-fashioned rules of the game in their day, when they were confined to half-court play, permanently stationed on offense or defense. But the joy of full-court freedom was the extent of our liberated thinking as seventh-graders learning layups. In fact, a number of us switched uniforms on alternating nights, trading shorts for skirts to cheerlead at the boys' basketball games. At the tender age of twelve, we were already learning to do it all.

We and our classmates nationally proceeded to higher education in record numbers. By 1982, women had outstripped men in the number of bachelor's degrees earned each year; by 1986 the same was true for master's degrees. In 1995, the proportion of women and men in the workforce who had bachelor's degrees was 23 percent and 20 percent, respectively.

Call us good daughters in an age of feminism. We were active and achievement oriented, eager to please and encouraged to excel. Life was full of opportunity, and it was hard to imagine it ever having been different. We grew up with all the benefits of a culture focused on equal opportunity but without a personal commitment to the egalitarian cause.

Today we may be "accomplished graduates of the Girl Project," as Whitehead says, but the funny thing is, no one exactly remembers enrolling us. Certainly not our mostly traditional mothers, who weren't making a feminist statement in signing up their daughters for summer soccer. Our dads were equally unwitting.

In general, when doors opened, we walked through. When asked why he wanted to climb Mount Everest, British mountaineer George Mallory famously replied, "Because it is there." In our lives as teenage girls, everything from basketball to band, soccer to student government, and debate to drama was *there*.

We got to adulthood by generally following the directions—directions that encouraged us to explore opportunities: do well in school, be well rounded, go to college (and the more competitive, the better). After graduating from college, most of us were eager to head toward the next frontier—marriage—but found out the road map isn't as clear through twentysomething territory.

The -Isms Don't Fit: Beyond Feminism and Traditionalism

Feminist is not a label that many of us claim, nor do we identify with those who drifted into man-hating dead ends.

A number of the women I interviewed tried to verbalize descriptions of their lives and outlooks that didn't fit neatly into either feminist or traditionalist categories. In part they were simply trying to put their finger on a paradigm that adequately portrays their own experiences, which aren't really representative of either camp. One woman described herself as a neotraditionalist. A few said they identified with aspects of both feminism and traditionalism, and a few others had no use for either tag.

Their comments imply that labels are in the mind of the beholder and may say more about that person's perspective than about the beliefs of the beheld. As one woman said, "At Harvard I was considered a raving right-winger; at my last church I was considered a feminist. I'm not a feminist; I want a man who is a leader. But if they want to think of me as a feminist because I think you should look at men and women with equal worth, that's fine. It's all in how you define these terms." In other words, the substance of one's belief is what matters, whatever others may call that. It's a sad irony that the movement intended to free women from the constraints of role labels has created new ones with which we must contend.

Our generation has been criticized by some feminists for being thankless free riders on the fruits of their labors, playing the sports we want to play, entering the schools and graduate schools of our choice, holding jobs and earning salaries that compete with men's in increasingly feminized work environments, with the media and pop culture applauding along the way.

Few things are really free, however, and the price some women feel they're paying today for the last generation's trailblazing is high tolls for women en route to marriage. While our feminist forebears were frustrated by barriers to fulfilling work, today we are frustrated by obstacles to lasting love, some of which seem to be the result of the feminist movement itself.

How Shifting from Autopilot to Power Drive Got Us Nowhere

One of the early upsets to the applecart was Betty Friedan's 1963 book *The Feminine Mystique,* which criticized a one-size-fits-all cultural conception of womanhood. Friedan found "a strange discrepancy between the reality of our lives as women and the image to which we were trying to conform."

Friedan wrote *The Feminine Mystique* after surveying her fellow alumnae of the Smith College class of 1942 on the occasion of their fifteen-year reunion. A freelance writer at the time, she was hoping to use their feedback for a magazine article, but the responses prompted a much deeper inquiry that led her to investigate why her former classmates, many of whom were housewives, seemed so unsettled, discontent, and empty. The problem, she determined, was that life had not met their expectations.

The feminine mystique, as Friedan called it, "makes certain concrete, finite, domestic aspects of feminine existence…into a religion, a pattern by which all women must now live or deny their femininity." She wanted women to ask deeper questions about the purpose of life and their identity in it, and not just to go through the motions.

The book is, in part, a manifesto against life on autopilot.

But after raising some helpful questions, Friedan essentially called for a power override of autopilot. She had brutal words for the role of homemaker, writing, "I am convinced there is something about the housewife state itself that is dangerous," and describing the housewife as consigned to "a comfortable concentration camp," overlooking the fact that women might prefer to be in the home because of a natural attachment to family.

Betty Friedan pointed out some serious problems about going with the cultural flow without deeper reflection. But she didn't offer alternative criteria adequate for today's young women who are seeking a sense of purpose in the choices they make about life. In destroying one foundation, however inadequate, the work of feminists like Friedan failed to give women solid ground on which to stand when evaluating their purpose and direction in life. Instead, power struggles and absurd interpretations of equality have left everyone, particularly women, unsure of their footing in the postfeminist world.

Liberation, power, and choice have been the feminist creed. But liberation to what end? Power for what purpose? Choice for what outcome? These are not ends in themselves, and for that very reason the feminist manifesto continues to leave women unsatisfied. Without a fixed reference point outside ourselves, it's tough to find fulfillment.

Why One-Size-Fits-All Doesn't Work for Life Plans

Feminists have tended to categorize women as a homogenous class—a trait mystery writer Dorothy Sayers found "repugnant." "What is unreasonable and irritating is to assume that *all* one's tastes and preferences have to be conditioned by the class to which one belongs," Sayers said in a speech to a women's group in 1938. "Are women really *not human*, that they should be expected to toddle along all in a flock like sheep?"

A woman should be accepted simply as a human being, she urged, "not as an inferior class and not, I beg and pray all feminists, as a superior class—not, in fact, as a class at all, except in a useful context. We are much too much inclined in these days to divide people into permanent categories."

We crave rating systems to categorize everything from school performance to the strength of Tylenol. Superlatives are even sometimes applied to callings (for example, woman's *highest* calling is to be a wife and a mother).

But God does not call women as a class. He calls us as individuals, to Himself and to particular situations. God doesn't have a one-size-fits-all life plan for women. He has us each on a custom-built track that leads toward His glory and shapes us to be more like Him along the way. Our highest calling is to love God and to live in obedience exactly where He currently has us.

Category-consciousness has no place in the kingdom of Christ. We are called as individuals and must answer as individuals. We live out the life of faith through the specific gifts, opportunities, relationships, and responsibilities God has given us. We are to pursue God rather than to aspire after an image of female strength and independence or an icon of domesticity carved with embellishments beyond what Scripture promises or prescribes.

"Christian culture in particular has this sense of marriage as the ideal. It's what we're all moving toward," says twenty-nine-year-old Sharon, who grew up in the Midwest. As a result, observes Sharon, young women develop a sense of entitlement to marriage, which leads to frustration and even bitterness if it does not come along.

A number of the women I interviewed were befuddled by the perception that marriage and family seem to be regarded by some in the church as the highest state in life, the most sanctified and sanctifying station. This view leaves singles feeling like outsiders or incomplete Christians. A woman from northern Virginia described growing up in the church this way: "I don't remember any teaching of what to do with your life if you're not married. It was always, whatever you're doing, it's just a substitute for the time until you get married."

The veneration of marriage can sometimes leave the impression that singleness is second-rate. It's important that esteem for marriage be joined with a clear message about the truth of our position as individuals—single or married—before Christ.

It's also important to distinguish between inherited tradition and essential biblical teaching about women, work, singleness, and marriage. Traditions will vary, and shifting economics and culture will lead to changes in how things "have always been done." God's Word, not our comfort with custom on the one hand or our attraction to innovation on the other, should be the standard for evaluating change.

God's work isn't bound by human tradition. Responding to His call to participate in that work, many women have walked through doors unexpectedly opened to them—not as a statement, but as a response. That's why some women are surprised to encounter the perception that they are career women, as though they were responding to a cause and not a call.

Four

Mistaken for a Career Woman

"I don't like the word *career*. It makes me think of the eighties and some power job where you wear a blazer and carry a notepad." Nancy sat up straight on the edge of her seat to impersonate the perky professional. "It's like *Nine to Five,* the Dolly Parton days!

"I feel like it's a label that takes all of you and puts you into this career path. We're all so much more multifaceted than that. Yeah, we have our job on the one side, but that could morph. People go back to school and change paths a lot more now. That's why I think it dates you when you say 'career.' I don't feel like that really applies to our generation.

"I so don't put the career label on myself," said Nancy. By New York norms, Nancy is perfectly average as a thirty-three-year-old, single graphic artist. "But it's funny…when I go home to the South, all of a sudden I start to feel like this career woman."

Perceptions like that can create doubt that we're doing the right thing. Women who never wanted to do the vocational track in the first place now find that they are perceived as career women, which only seems to distance them further from the marriage track. It's a Catch-22. "Everything done by a woman who's not chasing men or having sex seems to make it harder, ironically, for her to find a man in the end," observed Bridgett, a thirty-six-year-old Washington DC woman.

Because of such misconceptions, some women don't like revealing the details of their professional lives to people they don't know well. They don't want to be reduced to the caricature of a career woman.

"I don't advertise my partner status in the firm because it gives people the wrong idea—that I'm defined by my career, that I'm aggressive, that I'm rich," said Ashley, a thirty-five-year-old attorney.

Twenty-nine-year-old Ellie, in a management position at a federal agency, said the same: "I don't like telling people what my title is. I want them to get to know me, not to make assumptions on the basis of my title or job—it's a very small part of who I am. Both men and women seem to get intimidated and pull back when they find out what I do. If they would talk to me for five minutes, they would know I'm not like that. I'm a down-to-earth, real person—not a big title on a business card."

A couple of women pursuing advanced degrees said the same thing about holding back their credentials. A student on the PhD track in theology at an evangelical seminary in the Midwest commented that people typically assume she is studying for a master's in counseling. She doesn't volunteer her academic portfolio early, especially with men. "When to play that card," as she put it, is always a tricky question.

Me, Intimidating?

Almost one in five women who responded to my online survey said they had been told directly that it is their fault they are not married because they are too intimidating or intense. More than half said the fact that men find them intimidating was a common obstacle that has kept them from dating or forming lasting relationships.

"Some of my guy friends have even told me, 'Well, you Washington career women are so intimidating,'" reported one woman in her forties. "We have these well-paying jobs, we own our homes, we travel internationally. But we're just living our lives fully, and we want to excel professionally. What do they expect us to do? I want to convey that I am professional as well as feminine and traditional. But men don't believe that all the time."

Some women worry that their educational and financial choices might be interpreted in ways they don't intend, signaling disinterest in marriage and motherhood. That concern about perceptions can add anxiety when it comes to decision making about everything from graduate school to buying a home.

For most women, getting a college degree is just a matter of course. Deciding whether to pursue a graduate degree becomes more complex. In chapter 3, Emma's decision at twenty-four not to go to med school in part because she wanted to get married and have a family is an example of how early we start wagering on the time line to marriage. Now, at age thirty-three, she's pursuing a PhD in nursing and is still single.

Then there's the decision about whether to rent or buy when it comes to housing. Extended singleness requires a roof over one's head, and buying has financial merits. Still, some women admit they were reluctant to commit to real estate, wondering if they were signing a mortgage or a moratorium on marriage.

A House for a Hope Chest

In generations past, a girl's dreams of marriage would be tangibly stored up in her hope chest. Mother and daughter would tuck away linens and other household finery—some of them homemade goods or family heirlooms—in a wooden trunk to be carried with the young woman into a new home following her marriage. The whole tradition, including the term *hope chest,* marked an expectant and practical orientation toward marriage.

Today, relatively few of us can sew much beyond a button or a hem, let alone an entire quilt, and the finer homemaking arts have largely died to the availability of mass-produced commercial goods that fill bridal registries at Crate and Barrel or Target. By the time we reached marriageable age, we Gen X women were more likely to have stored up trendy clothes, a music collection, and a modest library of academic knowledge than a household starter kit. For the modern woman, "her hope chest is now her brain," says anthropologist

Lionel Tiger, and her "dowry" is the "credentials and skill carried around in [her] skull." Some of the women carrying around credentials like MA, JD, and PhD, however, may be wondering if an old-fashioned dowry of three acres of land might have been more attractive to a man than three degrees, and if a girl with a nice, tidy cedar hope chest would fit more comfortably into his life than a woman with a home of her own.

But it's not just men's impressions—women have their own reactions to deal with as well. When one woman in New York told friends she was closing on the purchase of a condo, she confessed she was downcast: "I never thought I would be doing this by myself, and you don't really think about how hard it is until you're actually going through the process. It just feels like it's making my singleness kind of permanent."

As a woman in Chicago put it, "Making deliberate choices toward self-sufficiency feels like an admission of defeat. It is admitting that there is no one to take care of me."

What's more, when it comes to a place of our own, most of us would like to have a man on hand for "the blue jobs," as my friend Dan calls them—killing mice, fixing leaks, relighting the furnace pilot light, not to mention dealing with loan rates and refinancing.

For my own part, it took me ten years of renting to warm up to the idea of buying a house without a husband. Even then I might have thought myself out of the decision had it not been for a forty-eight-hour whirlwind turn of events that got me across the threshold of buying a little bungalow from an air force officer leaving for Iraq the following day. It was an unmistakable just-do-it moment.

For others, closing on a home wasn't a big deal. Most women I interviewed said it simply made sense for them to buy when they did. Thirty-five-year-old Ashley has now owned two places and shrugs at the idea of buying a house. "It's like buying a pack of gum," she said.

Still, it takes some adjustment, practically and psychologically, for those who had expected to be doing this with a companion. One twenty-nine-year-old who recently bought a condo couldn't figure out why she felt depressed after she moved in. "Then I realized it was because I always pictured buying a home with a husband. Buying on my own meant admitting to myself (and to the world) that the husband may not be coming anytime soon," Ellie explained. "Since I figured that out, it's been fine. Sure, I have to learn a little more about maintenance and have to deal with the hassles on my own, but that's okay. My brother came and helped me paint the place, and I absolutely love it. I've gotten to know a few of my neighbors, and I enjoy having a space of my own where I can entertain."

But Ellie does have a little lingering concern that the condo just adds to her growing résumé of daunting features, which include graduating from a top university and holding a senior management post at a large agency. "I do sometimes worry that the first impression people get is that I'm independent and I've got a great career and a condo and all. Are they just assuming that that's what I want, and I chose that, and I don't want to be married?"

Ambivalent About Ambition

From their own perspective, these women are just doing what's been in front of them to do, putting to work the resources God has given them. They're surprised when others—especially men—perceive it differently.

Ellie's "great career" at a federal agency is actually something she never could have imagined or planned. As she describes it, she got a break working for someone in college and benefited from tremendous opportunities being alongside that boss over the years. But she is by no means wed to this track. Twice she thought seriously about leaving, and she doesn't know what she'll be doing a few years from now.

"I'm not good at long-term planning," Ellie explained. She thinks about going back to school, maybe in a completely different field—nutrition and health have interested her recently. Eventually she'll probably make her way back to California. "People are more relaxed there [than in Washington DC]," she said.

That's the kind of story I heard from numerous women who have spent a decade or more in the professional world. They describe themselves as driven, but not, in most cases, ambitious. For some, that term either had no relevance or made them recoil. They shrug off the idea that their job defines them. The more successful they are, the less interested they seem to be in talking about their professional status. Some are concerned that it will give the wrong impression about them or flatten their identity to one dimension. They tend to be more emphatic about their desire for marriage than their vocational aspirations.

SHE SAYS:
PROFESSIONAL WOMEN ON AMBITION

"Whenever God has something for me to do, it just falls into my lap. Or I have such a strong conviction about it that I can't *not* do it," reflected one woman at the head of an organization. "But I've never been an ambitious person. I've never had five-year plans and goals."

The following reflections from professional women profile their ambivalence about ambition, success, and their future in the world of work. Just as they couldn't see their path clearly up to this point, so also are they unclear about what the future holds for them—professionally or relationally. Most of all, they convey a sense that their professional paths have been guided by providence and not by their own planning. They recognize that professional success, like marriage, is ultimately out of their hands. Here is how they explain it:

I don't consider myself ambitious. People tell me I am, but I always associate ambition with a self-serving attitude that I don't want to be a part of. I jump at opportunities because they seem exciting; it's a desire for excellence and change. I don't like power. I don't like being in leadership, but I always seem to end up there; I have never chosen those positions.

(continues on the next page)

I've been very blessed to have mentors who see things in me that I have never seen. I trust them, and they convince me to try.

All the things along the way are opportunities that have arisen and I have not turned them down. I'm doing all this because I have no reason not to. It's scary and very overwhelming when I think about the responsibility, but wonderful that I can be making a difference.

—Sally, 34, PhD nurse

I haven't had crystal-clear career goals—there are several things I want to do, but I don't necessarily know what positions they entail. During college, the women who had the most interesting careers seemed to have gotten there serendipitously, not on a linear path, which was reassuring. I see that in my own path as well now.

If I were going to be single all my life, I feel like I should have accomplished more by now... I should be in Congress or a cabinet secretary, but instead I'm betwixt and between.

—Bridgett, 36, senior congressional staffer

I don't think of myself as ambitious, but I think others would say that I am. I have a deep desire to matter, to make a difference with my life. The Lord has given me some exceptional gifts, and I feel the weight of responsibility to use them for His glory.

That doesn't mean that I have to rise to a particular position, but it does mean that I'm not satisfied with the status quo, with just enjoying myself along the way. I want to know that the days I spend on earth are making a significant kingdom difference, and in the process of making that difference, I also hope to enjoy myself along the way.

—Andrea, 38, communications director
  in higher education

I never could have planned this path. There were lots of gaps, wilderness periods, where I had a feeling of uselessness: *God, why are You letting me flounder here like this?*

God has given me the confidence to do what I needed to do at the time. But I was a wallflower all the way through college.

I wasn't sure about taking the lead at my organization. A friend who is a businessman helped me work through it: "Where is the organization now? Where would you like it to be in three years? What can be done to get it there?" And after that exercise, I wanted to do it. It shifted the focus from me to the organization. It transformed the way I

(continues on the next page)

thought about it. Before that, I had focused on what I pictured the head of an organization should be: what initials they should have after their name, their accomplishments and experience—and I didn't measure up to that model. But this made me consider it in practical terms: what needs to be done, the technical aspects, the strategy—and it became a challenge that I wanted to take on. *I would like to help make this happen!* I thought.

—Pamela, 43, head of a nonprofit organization

I absolutely had career goals and was pretty driven and determined. Specifically, I wanted Jane Pauley's job or something along those lines.

Since that was a bit far-fetched and one of those "if you're in the right place at the right time maybe it will happen" kind of jobs, I didn't so much have a deliberate plan, but more the philosophy that success happened when preparedness met opportunity.

I've never just felt like I was on some career trajectory, but more as though I were following a certain path. When I came to that realization, I pretty much gave up the idea that I was in charge.

—Molly, 37, communications consultant

I don't know what *ambitious* means to people. I believe in doing things with excellence, and reaping the rewards—if reward is the right word. You do well what you're given to do.

I don't know why God has me where He does, but He seems to be granting me favor in the eyes of those around me and allowing me to be light there. Maybe it's so I can make a bigger statement by leaving it all one day.

—Ashley, 35, law firm partner

I'm not ambitious in terms of power or money or those kinds of things, but I do think I'm driven. I think my father was instrumental in giving me confidence. At an early age he would tell me what I'm good at: you can argue a point, you can speak in front of people, you speak eloquently and convincingly, you can negotiate. So I guess that helped spur me on to believe in myself and my skills.

I've been insecure in life generally, but I've always had confidence professionally. In social situations, maybe not, but in my work, I was young for what I was doing, I was different, but I always knew I was good at it, so I guess that's a gift.

—Sharon, 29, campus ministry leader

Flextime for Life: An Elastic View of the Future

If these women show some ambivalence about their professional futures, it shouldn't be interpreted as apathy. They can see lasting purpose in their current pursuits, even if they eventually walk away from what they're doing now. They can discern multiple strands of purpose weaving through the experiences of their lives.

"There's so much more going on in life that you can experience and pour your time and energy into than just what you do during work-hours," said Jen, a thirty-year-old living in New York. "I never would have chosen the current work I'm in. But now I see that God has given me all kinds of skills and knowledge that are good not just for the job today but also for wherever He's taking me.

"God is leading me somewhere—I don't know where, but that's not the important question. The thing I should be asking myself is, *Who am I becoming?* And I don't think I'm becoming just one thing—like a mother only. I am becoming the woman that God created me to be in work and family and relationships and experiences and challenges, setbacks and trials. There are so many things that are a part of who we are each becoming."

The idea of developing in many ways or of having multiple callings throughout life leads to an elastic view of the future. If life has veered from our expectations to date, one of the few safe assumptions we can make about the future is that it will continue to surprise us. Having an adaptable outlook on the days and years ahead will go a long way toward maintaining peace of spirit.

That flexible perspective applies to both work and marriage. Of the women I interviewed, those who have a decade or more of professional experience speak with a tone of flexibility about how work and marriage might interact in their future. They talk of "doing life together" in a marriage and of "reconciling callings" with a husband.

Bridgett, a senior staffer on Capitol Hill in her midthirties who has spent her professional years in public policy, can see things working out either for a more public life for her or for a situation in which she is supportive of her future husband's work, with them mutually deciding what that will look like. "If his job takes him to Italy for a year, then I won't be able to have such a public life...but Italy sounds like a lot of fun."

Even those who have been strongly committed to a career path seem willing to depart from it. "I've realized I'm not responsible for saving the world," said Molly, the thirty-seven-year-old who might have liked to vie with Katie Couric for a shot at being the first female evening news anchor. "I had such full and unique career and life experiences early on that I feel like I'm at a point where, if I got married and the situation were that I couldn't work, I would be fine with that. There's more that I can do and hope to do, but I don't *have* to."

Ellie had a similar outlook: "I'm sure there'd be some withdrawal if I left the work world, because you do get used to that cycle. But I find myself every year wanting the career less, and wanting these other parts of life more," she says. "It seems like without somebody in your life, the need to find a meaningful job is more acute. Still, we shouldn't get our purpose or worth from a relationship with a husband or boyfriend, or even a job; it should come from the Lord."

PART 3

Then and Now: What's Become of Romance?

Five

Closed Roads and Old Scripts

The three of us thirtysomethings, all single, sat around a dining room table on an overcast Sunday in late March for a lunch of left-over pizza, cold cuts, and Del Monte canned peas. Different turns have brought us to this particular weekend rest stop on the journey of life: Matt is divorced, Joe is widowed, and I've never been married. But our dissimilar paths are alike in one respect—they've all diverged from the road that rose to meet our parents when they were establishing families and households, the road we always thought we'd follow as well.

Each of us is the eldest child of parents whose lives followed the classic script for marriage and family. Their narratives begin on farms: a South Jersey dairy farm in the case of Matt's and Joe's mothers, who are two of four sisters, and a Western Kansas wheat farm where my father grew up, one of four children as well. Farm life was a no-fuss upbringing that deeply ingrained the Puritan work ethic in them. Life wasn't about finding yourself; it was about knowing God, making a living, finding a spouse, and having children.

Our parents left their family farms in the 1960s for Christian colleges, since they were good places to make progress toward those life goals. There they met and dated their future spouses, as did most of their siblings. Their first-date stories are full of the campus flavor of flirting in the library and dolling up for a winter banquet.

They all married before they turned twenty-five. Our fathers earned graduate degrees and became the family breadwinners. Our mothers trained for roles that were common for women at the time, teaching and nursing. It was work that they planned to set aside when they started having children. They were nurturers and supporters who stayed home to raise us and our siblings. It was the classic life script.

Our parents instilled in us the same aspirations for lifelong marriage, family, traditional roles, and a faith that would bind it all together. One way they cultivated these affections was by taking us back to their own roots, and the return to the farm—whether in South Jersey or Western Kansas—became a family ritual. In our young lives, the farm became a symbol of the first and most important things in life, the things worth returning to year after year, the things that gave stability, continuity, and meaning to life.

Every summer during my childhood my family would make a two-day trek in a Chevy Suburban from Chicago to Dodge City, split up by an overnight at an aunt's house in Kansas City. On the road, I spent hours mesmerized by the wheat fields passing by in a golden blur, a bobbing grasshopper oil drill occasionally snagging my gaze. Even as a child it made me wistful, but I couldn't articulate it then; I could only wonder at the sensation of space and time and age sweeping by between me and a fixed, far horizon.

Our parents wanted us to go to Christian colleges, at least partly in the hope that we, too, would meet spouses there. Of the twelve of us in our generation of the three families who have been to college, all of us did go to Christian colleges, but the old script didn't play out in the same way. Only two of the twelve met spouses there. Another two met spouses after graduation, and none of the rest of us have married.

For our generation, getting a professional start has been easier than establishing families of our own. In comparison to our parents' settled existence by this point in their thirties, we are more like vagabonds. They would have been sitting down to a Sunday pot-roast dinner with wedding-gift silver, not eating canned peas off paper plates with mismatched spoons.

But picking out china patterns together during senior year is no guarantee of marital bliss. At a recent gathering of college classmates, Matt's mother learned that all the other girls on her college cheerleading squad have divorced. An easier start doesn't guarantee a more carefree course, and the classic script doesn't necessarily lead to a happy ending.

My family's farm was sold after the deaths of both grandparents and the divorce of the aunt and uncle who had farmed it for almost thirty years. Matt and Joe's grandmother lived on the South Jersey farm until the day she died, six years after her husband's death. Her four daughters, their husbands, and nearly all her sixteen grandchildren returned for the funeral.

Matt and Joe have been talking all weekend about what their family should do with the farm. Joe's two children come out of the tent they made with blankets to join us at the table for our Sunday leftovers. Joe prays before the meal and alludes to the sermon we've just heard at church. It was about God overriding man's plans once again, telling King David, *No, not yet,* when he wanted to lay the foundation for a magnificent temple that would replace the portable Tabernacle. For a God who journeys with His pilgrim people along unexpected roads, a tent would house His presence and serve His purposes just fine. Kings and cultures have their traditions, but God doesn't always abide by them. The God of the unexpected wants a people ready to follow Him into the unexpected.

Still, we long for foundations of stone, the foothold of farmland, and the old roads to romance—forgetting that they signify something greater than themselves.

Learning from the Closed Road

It's pointless to pine for bygone conditions that made it easier for former generations to establish their own marriages. But while it profits a woman little to *long* for roads closed to her, it is wise to *learn* from them.

The generational shift in how many of us seek, and sometimes find, marriage has been dramatic. That shift can lead to frustrated mother-daughter discussions as each generation tries to understand the romantic era of the other. Increasingly, it's also the subject of scholarly attention, as some serious thinkers turn their attention to the topic of dating and marriage.

Among them are the very accomplished couple Leon and Amy Kass. Both teach at the University of Chicago; she writes on culture, he on subjects like cloning. Together, they have compiled an anthology on courting and marrying called *Wing to Wing, Oar to Oar*. The book seeks to help young people make sense and stability of romance in an era of any-which-way relationships.

Why would such an erudite pair take on the subject of romance? As they explain it, they had witnessed too many of their former students struggling to settle in to satisfying relationships. As observers, they were "profoundly saddened" that these members of younger generations "are in danger of missing out on one of life's greatest adventures and, through it, on many of life's deepest experiences, insights, and joys."

Their own entry to marriage was much less complicated:

Opportunity was knocking, the world and adulthood were beckoning, and most of us stepped forward into married life, readily, eagerly, and, truth to tell, without much pondering. We were simply doing—some sooner, some later—what our parents had done, indeed, what all our forebears had done.

Not so today.... Many of the young, and more particularly many of the young women, strike us as sad, lonely, and confused.... For the first time in human history, mature women by the tens of thousands live the whole decade of their twenties—their most fertile years—entirely on their own: vulnerable and unprotected, lonely, and out of sync with their inborn nature. Some women positively welcome this state of affairs, but most do not, resenting the personal price they pay for their worldly independence.

The old romantic regime allowed the Kasses and many others to step easily and expectantly into marriage like a rite of passage into adulthood. Since then, cultural changes like the sexual revolution, the divorce culture, and greater geographic mobility, have reshaped society and disrupted the old order. As a result, once predictable paths to marriage have become uneven and difficult to navigate.

A Damsel's Dilemma

"Men have a lot of assumptions about women," said twenty-nine-year-old Ellie. "The feminist movement not only changed that but changed them, so they would assume that I'm not looking for a man, or that I'm not interested, or that I'm already taken because of all these things."

Greater female independence in general seems to come at a price for the individual woman. Some women wonder if their professional success and appearance of "having it all together" give the impression that they don't need men or aren't interested in marriage. "Your income goes up, you can afford things you couldn't before, and I think that men have the perception, 'Well, she has everything she needs. What can I, as a man, offer her?'" said Ann, thirty-four.

Women could give a number of answers to that question, but their responses tend to fit in the category of companionship and intimacy, particularly on an emotional level.

"There is something men offer that isn't just financial or material—it's emotional support. If only they were able to realize that emotional support is something that very strong, independent women need," said thirty-one-year-old Jasmine, who works in Washington DC.

"Guys have a tendency to think that because I don't ask for help, I don't have emotions," said a twenty-nine-year-old who works for a beach volleyball association in California. "In my opinion, that's where I need the help the most, my emotional side."

"Tough is not who I am. I'm only that way because I've had to be, and it's a lonely place to be. If there is a guy who cares enough someday, maybe I'll let down my guard," said a woman in Chicago.

Women who have had to be self-sufficient for years find themselves in a difficult position: they want emotional support, but it doesn't appear they need it. Playing the stereotypical damsel in distress, however, is a *distressing* prospect to many of them.

"I struggle sometimes when I watch other women dumb themselves down, or see them play the role of women in constant distress in order to be more attractive to men. That's just something I'm not willing to do. How do they do it?" wondered Jasmine.

Women who have made what they consider to be valuable use of their single years don't see themselves needing to be saved from singleness, as they may have at a younger age when they had expected marriage to come along earlier. "The dream of marrying is different for me now than it was at twenty-three. It's not a rescue fantasy, to have someone save me from my life, but more like enriching my life," said thirty-nine-year-old Lisa. It's about complementarity.

Women want men to be gentlemen, yet some women realize that the habit of having to do things on their own makes them less attuned to accepting courtesies. A thirty-seven-year-old woman told about spontaneously inviting a friend over for dinner after church. The trash needed to be taken out, and he offered to do it, but she insisted it was her job and she should have done it earlier—only realizing on the way back up from the Dumpster that the gracious thing to do would have been to accept his offer.

Women—and men—find themselves trapped in the crossfire of the war between the sexes, which "women are on the way to winning, but the conditions of victory may not be agreeable," observes Lionel Tiger. "The armistice agreement may contain conditions no one wanted or expected."

That's a rankling prospect for women who have been conscientious objectors to the war between the sexes all along and who readily agree that things have gotten tougher for men. "We're struggling with what to do with all this opportunity in our lives. We're confused. How can men have any idea what to do with us?" wondered a thirty-four-year-old woman in Chicago who finds herself perennially wrestling with whether to stay in her law-firm job in The Loop, go to graduate school for literature, or move back to eastern Europe where she formerly worked with a Christian outreach organization.

Even some outspoken feminists concede that changes since our mothers' generation have not achieved optimal results when it comes to male-female relationships. "Little did I realize that the sexual revolution would have the unexpected consequence of intensifying the confusion between the sexes, leaving women in a tangle of dependence and independence as they entered the twenty-first century," writes Maureen Dowd, columnist for the *New York Times,* in her book *Are Men Necessary?* "The fewer the barriers, the more muddied the waters."

Everybody Loves Lizzy

It's not so much that a woman's career or accomplishments are turnoffs, I'm told by an authority on the matter, a bachelor friend of forty-four. He said, "The real question is, in the midst of all of that, does she communicate to the man that he is needed rather than a fun add-on to her life?"

The professional life doesn't do her any service in this regard. His diagnosis: working women have to function in a mostly masculine world; they take on masculine characteristics, and they get so used to functioning in a professional persona that by their thirties they can't turn it off.

He suggests that a man wants a woman more like Elizabeth from *Pride and Prejudice.* Lizzy is witty, sharp, engaging, and an intellectual sparring partner—no empty bubblehead or wilting wallflower—"but she's also *incredibly* feminine. She has an irrepressible joy of life, a lovely girlishness despite her abilities."

The intrigue of her character, as he tells it, is that she becomes indignant over what she perceives to be a haughty, dour manner in Mr. Darcy. "She shows a female passion for the nobility of life and things that matter, and she wants to challenge Darcy's hard edge," he observes. That's not unwelcome: "We want women to soften us."

Ironically, Darcy the suitor suffers along as ignorant of Elizabeth's softer side as any modern frustrated beau. He experiences sharp-tongued barbs rather than tenderness of spirit from her. When at last they do reconcile their feelings—in the novel's closing paragraphs—and Elizabeth asks him to retrace the steps of his affection, he acknowledges that he was completely befuddled by her lack of emotion or encouragement of his pursuit. She asks Darcy,

> "Why, especially, when you called, did you look as if you did not care about me?"
>
> "Because you were grave and silent, and gave me no encouragement."
>
> "But I was embarrassed."
>
> "And so was I."

It isn't only men who are attracted to Elizabeth. Women like her too. She's strong, the anchor of her rather pathetic family, which is headed by a disengaged father and a shallow, silly mother. She can't coast through life on her family's wealth or her looks (which don't compete with her sister Jane's), and her chief asset is at least part earned—a liveliness of spirit cultivated by reading and inquiry. That spirit awakens interest in the wealthy Darcy, whose first condescending marriage proposal Lizzy rejects in a dizzying verbal exchange that proves her every bit his match in rhetoric, intellect, and passion. In the long run, she compels Darcy's happy surrender to a relationship of equals.

That's a hefty dose of girl-power for the eighteenth century.

Elizabeth Bennet may be a 1790s' foreshadowing of the Girl Project graduate, with a skill set and interests that don't conform neatly to the feminine ideals of her day. She was not very accomplished at the pianoforte and didn't draw at all, but always had her nose in a book and loved nothing more than a long, solitary walk. That also produced in her a well-honed sense of self.

If there is something of the modern woman in Lizzy's character, her lessons in love might have contemporary application as well, perhaps explaining the story's revived popularity, including the 2005 film version starring Keira Knightley as Lizzy. Not willing to settle for empty form in marriage, Elizabeth rejects the hand of the clergyman, Mr. Collins, whose egoistic, obsequious personality she can't endure. She knows her romantic quest for a marriage made of love and wit may leave her unmarried. When sparks do begin to fly with Darcy, she is awkward, stubborn, and misguided in her judgments. Their interactions are full of false steps and misinterpretations.

Both Darcy and Elizabeth are naturally ill-suited to the pettiness of the social life surrounding them, but they do succumb to its pride and prejudice. Darcy arrogantly claims to have rejected class prejudice by deigning to propose to someone of Elizabeth Bennet's modest means; her refusal clearly points out his pride. Meanwhile, Elizabeth's own smugness gets a humbling when she learns of Darcy's quiet efforts on her family's behalf and recognizes that her early judgments of him were unjust.

This character development completes the portrait of Elizabeth. She is not only depicted as an ideal woman, but the audience also gets to know her in an ideal way—through the descriptions of the book's omniscient narrator (or the screenplay's effective rendering of the story). That gives men like my friend a perspective on Elizabeth that they don't have on the women around them in real life. As the audience, we like Elizabeth before Darcy does; throughout the plot, we get to see her behind closed doors when Darcy does not.

The novel closes with a remark about the affection that Elizabeth and Darcy felt for her aunt and uncle, the Gardiners, for having prompted the breakthrough in their relationship. The Gardiners' role was minor. During a road trip with Elizabeth, the Gardiners merely wanted to take a tour of Pemberley, Darcy's estate, while the master was supposedly away, and they refused to let Elizabeth (who was secretly afraid it would appear too forward if Darcy found out) talk them out of it. As a result, a pleasantly surprised Darcy encounters a mortified Elizabeth during their visit.

Elizabeth's fear of appearing to have taken the initiative is another characteristic that she shares with some women today, particularly women who want a man to take the lead in a relationship. What do men have to say about this female reluctance to give a hint of interest?

"There is nothing wrong or confusing about showing interest in a guy by being at the same place he is and going up to him to talk," said a thirty-three-year-old male lawyer who grew up in Atlanta.

"Women shouldn't get hung up on the idea that they can't take any initiative at all," said my friend who likes Lizzy. In his opinion, many women are too passive. "A woman can send signals in ways that are very feminine, mildly flirtatious, not violating her integrity, or invading the role of pursuer."

"Just throw me a crumb!" he appeals, with palms outstretched in a screen-worthy gesture of passion.

Six

Bartering at the
Have-It-All Bazaar

In contrast to relatively clear-cut romantic rituals of past generations, today's marriage-minded woman must navigate among lots of options she doesn't want in the hope of finding the one she does. Romantic socializing today is generally casual and noncommittal, geared more toward gratifying sexual desires than helping a woman meet a marriage-minded counterpart.

A twenty-first-century single woman is in a social market where she theoretically can have it all: education her way, a job her way, sex her way, even babies her way. The hook-up culture offers sex-without-commitment on demand; modern technology offers babies-on-demand without men (except for their small donation). You can pay for sex and purchase impregnation, but there is one major exception to the have-it-all rule: a happy, healthy, satisfying marriage doesn't come in a catalog.

Society doesn't offer much in the way of social support, either.

It's as though a barter system has replaced a currency-based system of exchange. Well-established expectations for romance used to mark the way clearly to the public contract-covenant of marriage. Now privately negotiated terms set by the two individual parties have largely replaced these expectations.

For most of us, shops with marked prices are much less intimidating than a marketplace or used-car lot where haggling is the accepted way of doing business. Bartering in an actual marketplace can be a confusing experience. When you enter a street market, the power dynamics between buyer and seller are unclear, and much of the communication is unspoken—and therefore prone to misunderstanding and manipulation.

Unless the expectations of both parties match up, a bartering scenario challenges the original intentions of each. Situations like these require an assertive personality to resist ending up with something one never wanted or paying an inordinate price for something with no long-term viability.

A 2001 report observed such bartering conditions at work in the relational dynamics on college campuses: "Because processes for mating and dating are not socially prescribed and not clear, women feel that they must make up their own rules as they go along." In these improv relationships, the individual couples determine their levels of sexual intimacy, exclusivity, direction, and purpose of their relationships.

Outside the influence of parents and family, unless a young woman has chosen some other arrangement for accountability, she negotiates her own relationship terms privately and independently. Dad is no longer around to intimidate boyfriends; mom won't ask embarrassing questions about what she doesn't know.

That's not to say the traditional romantic script can't or doesn't work; many couples still meet on campus, go on actual dates, and marry soon after college. Some still follow the classic roles and rules for romance. But even when a man and woman follow the old norms, it isn't because culture generally demands it of them. It's because either the couple on their own or through the influence of their immediate community has chosen to adhere to those standards.

Even dating cannot be assumed to be the same as it was in our parents' day. "Many people have different ideas of what dating is," wrote one survey respondent. Because of the lack of social scripts for dating, each person has his or her own assumptions. As a woman in her midthirties observed, "You never know as a woman the expectations you should have going into it. I find guys make assumptions often different from those made by women, and it messes everything up. Dating roles have changed so much, and nobody seems to define the roles." That leads to plenty of confusion.

Casual, Loose, Undefined, and Weird

"I dated him six months, and it was casual and loose and undefined and weird," Heather said of her last relationship, and the group of women around her nodded. A few snickered. Her description summed up the twenty- to thirtysomething social scene.

Heather is thirty-two, petite, blond, and beautiful. She is

an accomplished professional, is serious about her faith, and seems to have no problem attracting men. But, she said, "I keep dating these men who cannot step up to the plate and initiate those conversations."

By "those conversations," Heather meant the talk that defines the relationship, the talk that lets a woman know how a man feels about her and where the relationship is headed. It's not that a man is oblivious to the desire—even a young man can sense that a woman craves that knowledge—but his own tendencies seem to pull him in the opposite direction.

"Girls have different expectations—they tend to need to know *right* now *exactly* where things stand," said Mike, twenty-three. "In an ideal world, guys should take the lead in that, but the awkwardness of having the conversation, combined with not really being sure about the commitment, results in guys not initiating that conversation."

Heather resists the idea of pushing the envelope on the discussion, but the alternative is to go for months without clarity about where a relationship is headed, hoping that eventually the man will take the initiative. Often, she has waited in vain. Heather's Mr. Undefined-Weird, for example, would try to communicate things through joking.

"Four or five months into things, he called from a work trip to ask me, 'Can I tell the other guys that I'm with that we're dating?'

"I thought to myself, *You're calling me from Cairo, Egypt, to ask me if you can tell your friends that we're dating, and you haven't even told me whether we're dating or not? What is that?*

"He came back and dropped jokes about it a couple times, but we never had a serious discussion about it."

Heather's experience is by no means unique. A 2001 national survey of college women, *Hooking Up, Hanging Out, and Hoping for Mr. Right,* found that a woman usually had to ask the question or overhear the man defining the relationship to someone else before she knew where she stood with him. The study documents a lack of clarity about relationships coupled with a lack of actual dating on college campuses.

College women, the report found, had been asked on very few dates. Among seniors, only half had been asked on six or more dates over their four years of college; among all college women surveyed, a third said they had been asked on two dates or fewer since arriving on campus. Instead, the campus trend is hanging out or hooking up, which is defined as anything from noncommittal kissing to noncommittal sex: anything goes, so long as it doesn't obligate anyone.

The Death of Dating

This is not your mother's campus life. Members of Generation X— and now Generation Y—have grown up in an age "that lacks broadly recognized social practices and norms that help them to place their present desires and experiences in the context of their future marriages," concluded the *Hooking Up* report. Eight out of ten of the women surveyed said that marriage was an important life goal for them, and six in ten thought they would meet their future spouse before leaving college. But the campus climate doesn't seem favorable to helping them achieve that goal.

After college, lack of dating and lack of relational clarity continue. "I meet nice men, but have not been asked out in forever, and neither have most of my girlfriends," said Tricia, forty-one. "I'm not so progressive or independent that I'm willing to ask a guy out first, so therefore I wait, and I wait and I wait, which is hard for me at this point in my life." A woman in her midthirties told me that until a recent streak, she'd had just one date per year since moving to Washington DC five years earlier.

Marriage-mindedness can cause the dating environment to be all the more stressful in Christian circles by raising the stakes high from the outset. That self-consciousness can make it difficult to identify or establish common ground before applying marriage-oriented litmus tests to one another. Women express concern that friendly overtures to single men at church are misinterpreted because the environment is so charged with the overtones of marriage. "We need to establish friendships, but that's hard to do when men think you want to marry them because you're being friendly," said a woman in her early forties who's lived on both coasts.

"To give the guys credit, it's because the Christian culture puts so much pressure on marriage," suggested a thirty-four-year-old woman in Long Beach. What's more, if women get asked out only infrequently, when they actually do get a date, they "freak out," as a woman in Chicago put it. "The older we get, the more our hopes get tied up in any little thing," admitted a thirty-seven-year-old who attends a church on the East Coast, where she said nobody dates.

The natural progress of friendship is obstructed on the other hand by a sexualized culture: "Society is so sexually minded, it's very hard just to become friends, to get to know each other as persons," said one woman.

Navigating between the twin pressures of high stakes marriage-mindedness on the one side and a sexually charged society on the other is a difficult passage. It contributes to a mounting stress level that makes an intimidating situation all the more daunting.

He Says: Matter-of-Fact About Marriage

Despite these obstacles, the presumption that marriage will come along as a matter of course in adulthood still seems to be widespread. Just as young women seem to grow up thinking that autopilot will deliver them to Destination Marriage, so also do young men in their early twenties. As a thirty-one-year-old single man with three degrees put it, "I thought marriage would be just like graduation from college, this distant event that, if you just kept doing what you were doing, would pretty much fall in your lap." He and the other thirtysomething men whom I asked no longer think that way, but the younger men I interviewed do.

"I'm sort of crossing my fingers and hoping marriage happens," says Jeremy, twenty-three, with a bit of a shrug. "I go through phases where I'll read something and sometimes be thinking about it, but otherwise it's not really something I'm working on."

Mike, also twenty-three, observes that he doesn't exert the kind of mental energy and activity in pursuing relationships that he does in other areas of his life, particularly in his job. "I do think my picture is that marriage will just happen," he says.

Twenty-six-year-old Josh is beginning to have a different outlook: "I've gotten more intentional about finding a wife in the last year. It was mostly job stuff that was keeping me from it before. I have become a little more deliberate about finding 'the one.'" Even so, he admits to distractions: "But then I'll get frustrated and find some girl to casually date, just to date or to pass the time, and a month or two will go by, and I'll realize it's not going anywhere. Then I'll get back on track."

In postmodern American culture, just as there is no longer a clear social script that leads to marriage, so too there is no longer a universally recognized rite of passage that marks the beginning of adulthood. If becoming an adult is most often associated with getting married and having children, that leaves the threshold of adulthood blurry for singles.

"I always thought I would seem and feel more mature in my own head by now," Josh says. "Yeah, lack of marriage is probably a part of that. I'm still taking in more than I'm contributing. I feel like I should be becoming more established in my church, but the circumstances of my job, which has had me on the road and back and forth a lot, always make me feel like a new member."

"Today adolescence lasts until about thirty. Will Ferrell is all about the thirty-five-year-old acting like a college student," adds twenty-five-year-old Jesse.

These guys in their midtwenties have two images of what it means to be a man: One is a provider, contributor—an image of strength and leadership. The other is sedate, staid, and tied down. It's a double-edged sword, they admit, and that makes them just a little hesitant to embrace it. In the end they know they will, but they're not exactly rushing toward it.

Old roads gave the impression of leading inevitably to marriage, and perhaps they occasionally still do. But an increasing number of young men and women are arriving at the end of their twenties or thirties to find that marriage just doesn't come along as a matter of course. Finding our way along less familiar routes is part of the pilgrimage. That takes work, but not the nine-to-five sort.

Seven

Working at Romance

Sometimes relatives and friends at weddings or reunions will ask, "Why aren't you married?" How am I supposed to answer? It's not like I can just buy marriage off the shelf. You have to trust God with your circumstances. It's not something you just decide to do one day when you're supposedly ready.

—SHARON, 29

For women who are deliberate, driven, and goal-oriented in their work and other areas of life, lack of success in reaching Destination Marriage comes as a surprise—not just to us, but also to Aunt Polly and the others who pepper us with questions at family functions and other social gatherings. When other doors have opened easily, it's bewildering that the door leading to marriage has been hidden or closed to us.

Frustrated by that lack of success and the confusion of the barter system, some singles are seeking strategies to better manage life outside work. The growing popularity of online matchmaking and speed-dating are two examples of a desire for structure in an otherwise ambiguous romantic world.

Internet matchmaking uses serious math to try to predict romantic chemistry; answers to questionnaires are plugged into algorithms to identify matches. Companies like Perfectmatch.com and eHarmony.com hire psychologists and scientists to determine the essence of a good match.

Speed-dating introduces time management strategies to the dating scene. For example, 8minuteDating.com is all about efficiency: eight dates, eight minutes each, at a single event, for about thirty-five dollars. BriefEncountersUSA.com gets things done even more quickly. Participants spend three to six minutes conversing before the bell rings for them to switch partners. At the end of the event, each person indicates which of their interviews they'd like to pursue further. Within forty-eight hours, contact information is e-mailed to those whose interests are mutual.

The Golden Rule Applies to Romance Too

Not only are Internet dating and speed-dating setting up new rules in the world of relational bartering, but they are also providing some coaching along the way.

Brief Encounters gives participants advice about how to have an enjoyable and successful evening meeting people. It turns out to be pretty solid counsel, the kind your mother might give you. It begins with a variation on the Golden Rule ("Care more about the person sitting across from you than you do about yourself"), gives some helpful hints ("Smile and make eye contact...leave your baggage at home"), and suggests questions that will help participants get to know the other person beyond first impression.

Then there are a couple of tips aimed at the barter-scarred—those who have had too many overtures fail in the no-rules world of dating today. One tip is for the results-oriented, type A person who is inclined to raise the stakes too high: "Act as though you have nothing to lose.... The fate of the Western world isn't at stake, nor is the fate of the rest of your life."

Another piece of advice is for those who have been burned to the point of apathy: "Be 'at stake.' This means be totally, completely, 100 percent responsible for your experience with the person seated across from you."

That kind of advice—urging personal responsibility and other-centered interaction—sounds a lot like what a Sunday-school teacher might have told you about life in general. Turns out the Golden Rule is the secret behind any human relationship and our responsibility no matter what the situation.

Throwing Expectations into a Cultural Melting Pot

A cultural melting pot like New York City has no regard for individual assumptions about the way romance is supposed to work.

"Marriage isn't on the mind as much here in New York, so there isn't that pressure you feel other places," says Sharon, twenty-nine. "Here, it's totally normal not to be dating. But when I go home to Minnesota for Christmas and see high-school friends, the questions are all about dating and marriage. It seems weird to them that I'm not dating anyone. Sure, I want to get married, but I'm okay with this job and my life here, and that just seems boring to them. So then I start thinking, *There must be something wrong with me.*"

Kimberly nods as well. She and Sharon grew up in the same town. Sitting with two other friends, Jen and Nancy, in Jen's high-rise apartment on the city's northeast side, they're telling me about single life from a New York perspective. Sharon and Jen were both enamored of the city as teenagers. Kimberly moved here for a cause—she teaches middle school in East New York–Brownsville. Nancy is the lone exception: she didn't want to come to New York at all.

"I was flat-out, *No thank you!*" she recalls. "The people were crazy, and I wanted a job somewhere warm." Nancy grew up in Atlanta, where she attended a prep school just as two generations before her did. But she decided not to follow in her family's footsteps and pursue an Ivy League education; instead, she studied sculpture at a Virginia college and later went to design school. After that she surveyed her options and realized that a job offer beckoning her to New York was too obvious to ignore. Seven years ago, at the age of twenty-six, Nancy changed her mind and moved to the city.

"I actually feel fear when I anticipate leaving New York—if I ever do," admits Jen. She's from a small town in Wisconsin, where her ideal of marrying at age twenty-eight was already well higher than the norm. Now she's thirty. "I feel fear that all of a sudden thoughts about not dating or being married will be at the forefront of my mind and I won't be able to just go about normal life without being confronted with it constantly."

"If I leave New York, I have to get married *immediately*—next boy who crosses my path," jokes Nancy, who does plan to move back down South someday. "I'd just feel so out of place!"

Sharon moved out of the city two years ago to a nearby college town where she works in campus ministry. "Even now that I live in the suburbs, I feel a little more like the odd woman out. It's harder to find community as a single because so many of the access roads to it are couples focused—there are couples Bible studies, couples classes, and marriage groups. In New York, it's a no-brainer to find community. Married, single, dating, not dating, whatever. Community is so much easier in the city."

Sunk back in a leather recliner, Nancy is trying to figure out what accounts for the city culture's ultracasual approach to dating. "I think that part of the reason it's so laid-back here is a pronounced equality between men and women that sort of strips away tradition and expectations and assumptions. When you think about traditional dating, where boy meets girl, and boy takes initiative and asks girl out, picks her up in the car, walks her to the door…well, New York just is not that lifestyle. Guys don't even have cars!

"Traditional roles just don't fit here. There's no expectation for women to be pretty and dainty. Yeah, we all wear our dainty little shoes in the summer, but they get scuffed up on the street, and you step in a puddle, and there are rats running everywhere."

"It's so diverse. No one's abnormal... There is no normal," says Kimberly. "It pushes back against all kinds of assumptions."

"When you meet someone, you're up-front: 'This is who I am, who are you?' It's almost like you circle each other," says Jen, motioning to illustrate two points tracing each other in orbit. "There's not an assumption of common ground. Even as Christians you have some common ground, but it's still work."

"Things don't come easily here. You have to fight, you have to think, you have to stretch," adds Sharon.

"New York is a place where we all get a little bit introspective—maybe a little bit too much," says Nancy. "We're all being challenged and constantly changing. In New York I have experienced growth in all directions, in areas I didn't even know could grow and expand and be challenged and be threatened." She's trying to sculpt the dimensions of that change with her hands as she talks. "I had convictions when I came here that I no longer have, and new ones that I've picked up along the way. I really think this city brings out the gunk; stuff rises to the surface because you're always bumping into people—"

Kimberly nods. "Yeah, you live with roommates because you can't afford your own place."

"There's no room to get away from people—ever," Jen adds.

"It's on a physical level down to your soul and your spirit," Nancy concludes. "Living here reminds me of God heating up the fire so that all our impurities and imperfections—all that dross—rise to the surface and get scraped away."

Overthrowing Idol Expectations

Whether we're single in New York at twenty-eight or married in Nebraska at twenty-four, God uses all kinds of conditions and circumstances to mold us in His image, and He rarely restricts Himself to our expectations. Our plans tend to end up in the pile of dross.

"I never thought I would be single at thirty-seven. I thought I would be married and be done having children by now," said one woman, and a number of others echoed her in similar comments.

Fill in the blank: *I never thought I'd be...*

Jilted at twenty-seven?

Unemployed at thirty?

Our expectations seem to create serious blind spots to God's purposes in our lives, since His work often appears aimed at removing them so we can see Him. The crucible of sanctification melts away illusions of self-sufficiency and makes us know our need for God's goodness, not as mere truism, but as tangible, gut-checked certainty. It makes us realize God's work of redemption isn't a cold abstraction; it is a force that reshapes us through the friction of frustration, even despair, until a humble, reconciled peace can grow into joy.

"I was screaming at God the other day. It was a really violent prayer," said Jackie, twenty-eight, a graduate student in Chicago. She was speaking in the wake of a broken relationship that once looked like it would head toward marriage. "In the midst of that, all of a sudden, something in me actually thanked God that I didn't marry Paul, because I know I'm exactly where I'm supposed to be now.

"I do actually like my life right now, but it made me mad to admit it. I have this picture that I should be miserable since things aren't the way they were supposed to be—they aren't what I wanted them to be. I'm good at miserable, I do that *really* well…I'm less good at being peaceful where I am.

"Getting dumped completely threw off everything I thought my life would be like. It was one big shake that made me seek to figure out what I'm doing with my life. And now I feel like I'm finally making some directional progress toward becoming the woman that God has called me to be."

A bitter breakup is one of those experiences that will make us think long and hard about what makes us get up in the morning. At times like that, getting lost in work or activities or some other distraction is a tempting short-term fix. Ultimately, however, there's no substitute for finding the sense of purpose that outlasts boyfriends and keeps us on course through the tailspins of life. That's what it means to have a call from now to not yet.

PART 4

A Call from Now to Not Yet

Eight

The Sense of Callings

Ask a young woman in her midtwenties to picture herself single ten years in the future, and her heart will likely sink at the prospect (see the answers I got to that question in chapter 2). But what if that fear becomes a reality? What if singleness sticks around until she's into her thirties—or even beyond? How will she be content while one of her major life goals remains unaccomplished? What should she do in the meantime?

Life in-between shouldn't be killing time or spinning wheels. Women like Carli, Emma, and Hilary—who are on the other side of that decade of singleness—convey what it's like to have a sense of purpose in-between. These women share some striking characteristics. Each has walked single for a decade or more, wrestling with her own expectations and those of others while dealing with the practical questions of life on her own. She may spiritually and emotionally struggle with being single at times, but she has found contentment in her present circumstances while hoping for something more. She is living with a heart poised between now and not yet. Here's a closer look at her profile:

- *She lives deliberately.* She is intentional about choices in life, from work to church to friends. She wants to use her gifts to make a difference, both now and in the future. She feels frustration when she observes others not being deliberate about relationships or even life in general.

- *She is reflective about her experiences.* Her struggles have made her evaluate herself, and she uses her experiences to smooth rough edges or to adjust course. She generally owns her faults and talks about men and relationships with a gracious and measured tone; she is sometimes disappointed but isn't grudging. She is reconciled to life circumstances that haven't worked out exactly the way she might have wished.

- *She seeks balance in her life.* Variety characterizes her interests, pursuits, and relationships. She may have had to learn it the hard way through burnout, but her life is about more than her job.

- *She knows her vulnerabilities and makes choices accordingly.* If she recognizes a tendency toward loneliness, bitterness, or jealousy, for example, she takes steps to avoid or overcome it. She may keep a full schedule of meeting friends, choose not to live alone, or avoid spending too much time around others who are bitter about their singleness.

- *She views life as an adventure, not a pity party.* She does not think that she's missed out on life. She has enjoyed the freedom to travel, to pursue her own interests, and to set her own priorities. While she wants others to recognize the struggles of singleness, she doesn't want others to pity her as though her life were incomplete.

- *She takes reality in stride.* At times, unexpected challenges demand her attention, from family crises to medical issues. "Life intrudes, and you just deal with it," said one thirty-nine-year-old who recently had to help her single mother through a serious illness.

- *She continues to hope for marriage.* She doesn't hide her desire, but she doesn't pine for it either. She is seeking marriage to deepen her life, not to escape it.

- *She has an elastic view of future married life.* She thinks outside the box about how marriage, family, and work would fit together for her, especially as childbearing years wane and professional expertise accumulates. She is not adamant about keeping a career; in fact, she may be quite ready to be done with it. But she can probably picture a whole spectrum of choices that she may not have seen at twenty-two. She views marriage as a partnership, a process of reconciling callings. If she is to marry, it will be to a man she respects, whose leadership she esteems.

- *She is encouraged by what God has done in her life.* She sees purpose in the course her life has taken, even in unexpected singleness. She may realize she would not have been as ready to marry at twenty-three as she thought she was, or that she could not have imagined the places God has taken her or the ways He has stretched her, but she is glad for how she has changed as a result. Singleness has strengthened her spiritual life, and she may even marvel at the way God has used it for her good and the good of others.

- *She has a sense of purpose anchored in God.* Life has sometimes shifted unpredictably, and she may be unclear about what she'll be doing a few years down the road, but she has a "go with God" mentality that gives her a sense of security, contentment, and even joy. She has developed an outlook that life is a pursuit of multiple callings; the specific conditions may change, but her life is all on track.

What does it take to have that sense of contentment and direction? To begin with, an understanding of God's call, which transcends current circumstances.

First Call

As human beings, we have a strong sense that we were born for a purpose, that our existence is linked to something beyond our own physical frame and material surroundings. One metaphor that the Bible uses to describe that link to the transcendent is *call.* God's call is an expression of affection for us and desire for us to reciprocate that love. When that call stirs a response in us, it is an acknowledgment of both need and desire for God: We admit that nothing in or around us can satisfy us completely and eternally. We acknowledge God and His work through Christ as the source of all we lack and need, both now and for the future.

Responding to that call is a commitment to love God, to know Him, and to seek to become more and more like Him. Our relationship with God becomes the source of identity, belonging, direction, and purpose when we feel rudderless or lost at sea.

Identity

Responding to God's call gives us a sense of identity. Our value is in Him because of what He has done for us and not from what we do or what we are by nature, marital status, education, or employment. This identity should show up in our character and actions—in the things we think, say, and do. Our lives should bear an imprint of Christlikeness.

Our status in life, whether marital or material, may change, but our status in Christ will not. Our value in Him should anchor our identity and shape our self-image through all the phases of life, including singleness.

Belonging

God is not a force or a state of being. He relates to us personally. When God calls us, He calls us into a relationship with Himself, the kind of close relationship that implies a sense of belonging to each other.

To help us get a better feel for what it means to belong to a transcendent yet personal God, the New Testament uses vivid, tangible images to describe the relationship. Jude writes his New Testament letter "to those who are called, wrapped in the love of God the Father and kept for Jesus Christ" (verse 1, NET).

Elsewhere we are described as "beloved" and as those He calls "by name." Corporately, the church is called the bride of Christ, a metaphor that gives us a deeper sense of belonging to God and to fellow believers. These descriptions of belonging and companionship assure us that whatever our phase of life, we are not navigating alone.

Direction

When our identity is anchored in Christ and we have a sense of belonging to Him, He becomes the reference point by which we set the course of our lives.

A driver's education instructor makes a point of telling fifteen-year-olds that if they don't keep their eyes on a point well down the road before them, they'll constantly be overreacting to things immediately in front of them and end up weaving around like a drunk driver.

Similarly, at twenty-five or thirty-five, if we're not fixed on an eternal reference point, decisions made under the influence of a momentary mood can send us on an erratic course through life.

Purpose

What a person *is* determines what she *does*. Because our identity comes from our relationship with God, so does our purpose: to glorify and enjoy Him. All aspects of our lives are to be integrated into that purpose: "So whether you eat or drink or whatever you do, do it all for the glory of God" (1 Corinthians 10:31).

We are also told to "live a life worthy of the calling [we] have received" (Ephesians 4:1). Our everyday habits should reflect the fact that we are connected to a holy and transcendent God, to His work here on earth, and to something beyond the here and now—beyond today's to-do list, less-than-ideal circumstances, or current mood. The way we walk through life should give the impression that we live for a purpose not only present but future, that we are living life poised between now and not yet.

Personal Callings

The calling to Christ isn't just spiritual abstraction. God calls us, and we answer within the here and now of our everyday lives. That means that in all the ambitions and activities of life, we should seek to be like Christ, to obey Him, to glorify Him, and to enjoy Him and His creation. The specific ways in which each of us does that are our personal callings.

Our callings are all around us. Our current circumstances and situation—gifts, relationships, responsibilities, opportunities, location, limitations, singleness—are parts of God's purposes for us. These add up to the sum of our callings. This is where God wants us to be at this time so we learn to be like Him, to live in obedient faith, and to experience all the joy He has for us now.

We live out our first call to God in many ways throughout the seasons of life, so it is appropriate to think of these ways as multiple *callings.* Using the plural distinguishes these personal callings from the singular purpose of our first call to love and serve Him. These personal callings may change, but our first call to Christ will not. In each circumstance of life, we are to glorify and enjoy Him.

The idea of multiple callings should also help us escape the trap of elevating any one earthly purpose above all the others. That place of highest, first call is reserved for the pursuit of God. To let another role or relationship become the sole focus of life is to ignore the many ways in which we are to live faithfully before God and see Him at work in our callings.

While today's particular task might seem quite ordinary, it's nothing short of extraordinary that the ruler of the universe would fashion the mundane details of our lives to accomplish His purposes for each of us. These are the fingerprints of a great mystery working itself out in our lives: how the supernatural infuses the natural course of our lives, how the will of God gives wide space to our human will to accomplish His ends for each of us.

Each new day, this cosmic choreography plays out in the setting of individual lives: God working out His purposes, and each of us working out the life of faith, all within His grand orchestration. Everyday existence is the adventure of discovering where this dance of life will lead and what it will make of us in the meantime, even if it isn't the particular step or tempo we thought we'd be following. Knowing that the stutter-steps and unexpected dips are a part of God's callings for us gives us reason for contentment and confidence in our next moves.

Nine

Called to Contentment:
Living Happily, Here and Now

Our calendars can fill up quickly. But it's easy to feel empty in the midst of a full life if there's no sense of purpose in the busyness. Is the whole of life more meaningful than the sum of its parts?

What we choose to do in life is important, but *why* we choose to do it matters too. We can be slaves to circumstance, to feelings, or to what others might think. We can look at the daily schedule as simply passing the time until we get to something better in life. Or we can approach life as an ongoing occasion to be good stewards of what we've been given. We can be intentional in our responsibilities and relationships and be on the lookout for the opportunities where we can best put our gifts to work. That's what it means to discern and pursue our callings. With that outlook, our everyday duties and activities contribute like a paycheck into a lifetime account of contentment.

To Be Called Means Life Is Not Just About Us and Our Self-Actualization

When life planning begins with personal fulfillment as its principal objective, it is unlikely to achieve that goal. Yet that's exactly what much contemporary counsel for women suggests that we do: fulfill ourselves through work, fulfill ourselves through mothering, or fulfill ourselves through a combination of both. The advice often boils down to a tail-chasing pursuit of self-actualization.

To look at life as a set of callings from God is a radically different perspective than that of self-fulfillment. Life isn't about finding ourselves; it's about glorifying God. When we're focused on living purposefully by following God through our personal callings, we're less likely to be distracted by the yo-yo effect of current fads about how to find fulfillment.

Our callings in life are *from* God and *for* others. Our talents are to be used in obedience to God rather than in self-aggrandizement. Ultimately, nothing brings greater personal satisfaction than pursuing our callings for His eternal purposes.

A Sense of Callings Connects Our Pleasure with God's Pleasure

"God is most glorified in us when we are most satisfied in him," says Christian teacher John Piper. Linking God's glory to our satisfaction sounds like some epicurean "eat, drink, and be merry" philosophy. *Carpe diem.* Could that be Christian?

Living by callings means that we are living in the paths that God created for us. We are seizing today to make the most of the opportunities God has given us in this moment. By answering His call in these ways we show esteem for God. Honoring God, in turn, brings us pleasure—just as we take joy in honoring those we love here on earth.

To live by callings means to enjoy God's glory. To delight ourselves in the Lord means to take pleasure in seeking God, knowing Him, and worshiping Him. This leads to greater appreciation for His character, His company, and His work.

We go through this same taste-training with other things in life, from fine wine to classic opera to sports. Not many of us are born loving the finest and most complex things—Pinot Noir doesn't trigger the same taste response as Pepsi, and Verdi isn't as accessible as eighties rock. Even as adults, we fail to give due credit to things we don't understand or haven't taken the time to learn about. During the last Winter Olympics, I realized my lack of appreciation for the complexity of some of the sports, one of which was curling. Now, I know nothing about curling and would not bother to watch it on my own, but I was with someone who understood the sport and could explain why the curlers were barking at each other and what the furious sweeping of the ice with brooms was all about. On another occasion I was watching figure skating with someone who actually had skated and could tell the difference between a triple and quadruple axel. While I can appreciate figure skating even as an uninformed spectator, I cannot spot a quadruple axel.

Tuning our appreciation to these less accessible things—spending time learning about their characteristics and the qualities that distinguish them—is a gratifying experience that introduces us to new types of enjoyment. Some are more worthwhile than others, and curling still isn't at the top of my list. But there is nothing more profoundly satisfying than getting to know what God is like and appreciating more deeply the way He interacts with us.

Understanding Life As a Set of Callings Provides Balance

Callings don't fit on a time sheet. This isn't about forty hours a week; it's about all-the-time overtime. In some seasons of life, paid work may be among our callings, but it won't be our only calling. The whole fabric of our lives is made up of callings from God—family relationships, friendships, community connections, and civic responsibilities. That perspective is an important one to have on either side of "I do," so the sooner we learn it, the better.

If we recognize that callings include an entire network of relationships, responsibilities, and opportunities in life, we will be more likely to keep work in proper balance with the rest. "One can take a job seriously precisely because one does not take it too seriously," observes ethicist William F. May.

Understanding this also helps to avoid the trap of workaholism. Work-hours can easily bleed into the evening when there isn't a family at home to make us observe the dinner hour. Working hard is one thing, but when a job begins to edge out other priorities and relationships, that's a problem. Of course, we rarely intend to let a job consume the rest of our lives, but this can easily begin with the lofty but mistaken view that a particular employment or cause is one's sole calling from God and that all else in life should take a backseat to it. A single job is never the whole of one's callings.

Callings are from God, and that is what gives them dignity—not the pay grade or the credibility that comes attached to them.

Having a Sense of Callings Stops the Nonsense of Competitive Life Comparisons

If I were to average the per-family kid count of friends' Christmas card updates last year, I'd say it's at about 2.5. It's easy to look at those family photos and feel way behind as a single woman.

Comparisons become moot and jealousy grows pointless, however, when we understand that there is no one else on this particular track. God's callings create a personal course for each of us, and what's important is how we run our own race. That also makes it possible to cheer on others as they run their different races (and happily post snapshots of their grinning cherubs on the refrigerator door).

If Each of Us Has Multiple Callings, Then We Haven't Missed the Mark if We're Not Married

One of the toughest parts of looking forward to marriage is wondering when it will come around. This year? Next year? Five years from now? *Ever?*

That's not a problem with callings. Discovering your callings isn't like being on hold, waiting for a second interview, or wondering if *he* will call. We don't have to wait around for callings to appear or wonder if we've missed them. They are made up of what God has put before us to do *right now,* such as pay back college loans, clean the house, finish that project at work, help a friend who's sick. And they are the opportunities we see emerging for *the future* that fit our skills and interests (that new position at the office, a master's degree in journalism, a chance to move closer to family).

That also means we don't have to worry that we've missed a calling—and that includes marriage. As long as we live attentive to the first call to Christ and the personal callings He has put in our lives, we can be confident that we aren't in a holding pattern just because twenty-five (or thirty, or forty) is around the corner and marriage is nowhere in sight.

A person's callings *may* include, but will not be limited to, marriage. Even for those who do marry, the marriage relationship is not the sum total of their callings. To reduce the idea of callings to a single relationship—even one as central and life-changing as marriage—is to miss the point. Getting married, in other words, shouldn't be the measure of any woman's success in life.

Marriage, motherhood, and the women in those stations of life deserve high esteem. But what makes wives and mothers admirable?

The woman who puts her faith in Christ finds her identity and value in Him, not in her marital or maternal status. A woman who is a wife and mother and who faithfully loves and serves God and her family deserves honor and praise for being faithful in the roles God has given her for that season of her life—not for the accomplishments of attracting a man, bearing children, or keeping house like Martha Stewart.

In the same way, the Christian woman who is single has value from her identity in Christ, not from her professional standing, heroic volunteer work, or footloose freedom. The practical way she shows her love for Christ is by obeying Him in the callings He has given her for this stage of life, including work, family, friendships, and service opportunities. If she is living faithfully in the callings God has given her and is open to what His hand might bring later, there is no reason for her or anyone else to think that she is incomplete or that she hasn't fulfilled her purpose because she is not married.

Our status in life—marital, economic, vocational—is part of God's purpose and should therefore be a source of contentment rather than anxiety. Contentment doesn't mean we have to be passive and let life roll past us, though. We should each be making "directional progress," as Jackie in Chicago said, to become the women God has called us to be. Our personal callings play a part in showing us that direction.

Ten

Callings as Catalyst and Compass

A young woman may have a whole world of options in front of her, but if the only career she ever wanted was motherhood, what's the difference between all the other choices? Is teaching or accounting a better option? In the seasonal doldrums of singleness, does it matter whether you live in Detroit or Denver? For a heart set on marriage, other choices can sometimes seem pretty uninteresting and arbitrary. In the absence of better criteria for choosing, decision-making junctures can make us guess on the time line to marriage or leave us angling to better our prospects of meeting Mr. Right. But if we are conscious of our callings when we evaluate choices, we will be equipped with a more certain source of motivation and direction.

Callings Give a Sense of Direction to Our Lives

Like a compass needle pulled toward the magnetic force of the North Pole, our first call orients us toward God, shaping our personal callings and helping us develop a sense of direction for life. Building an actual compass is simple enough for a fourth grader. It has two essential parts: a magnetized needle and a bearing that can move without friction (like a cork floating in water).

Creating an internal compass for life is trickier than building a science fair submission, but there are parallels between the two. It begins with a clear line of thinking, fixed on God and free from friction created by emotions, circumstances, or misplaced desires.

This sense of direction is the insight and intuition that come from knowing God and knowing oneself. Getting to know God means getting to know what He's said through His Word, the Bible. Scripture makes clear its purpose to help equip us for life, telling us what God thinks, describing the kind of life He expects of us, and honing our own judgment (see 2 Timothy 3:16–17).

Understanding Our Callings Equips Us to Make Decisions

When faced with a choice, like whether or not to accept a job offer that will require a move to Denver, we don't have to be incapacitated by indecision. We have better criteria for decision making than flipping a coin about where we have the best chance of meeting a mate or guessing at how long it will be until we're married.

We should be looking at how God has made us, what gifts and responsibilities we have, and how those mesh with our opportunities to serve Him and others. We should constantly be developing the habit of taking our inventory. By doing so, we'll be equipped with adequate criteria for decision making, whether we are dealing with an unexpected layoff or acceptance letters from three different law schools.

Renewing our minds is an ongoing project that is cultivated by resisting reflexive conformity to cultural expectations. By fixing our attention on God's call, we develop a perspective that looks at the world as God's stage for working out His kingdom purposes, and we learn to discern our part in that.

Scripture directly links this transformation of our perspective to our ability to discern God's purposes: "Do not conform any longer to the pattern of this world, but be transformed by the renewing of your mind. Then you will be able to test and approve what God's will is—his good, pleasing and perfect will" (Romans 12:2).

A Sense of Callings Gives Coherence to Life

On a recent Christmas vacation, my family visited relatives in Sterling, Kansas, "population twenty-five hundred friendly people," as Uncle Paul puts it. Cooper College was founded there in 1887, and today it's known as Sterling College with an enrollment of about five hundred students. Sterling was originally plotted as Peace, Kansas, but this is one college town where it's hard to imagine an antiwar demonstration ever taking place, either in 2006 or when my parents attended there forty years ago.

Kansas represents my roots, where I was born, where we have visited family nearly every year of my life. Today I live outside Washington DC, where we plan our routes to work around protests and security barricades and pass twenty-five-hundred unsmiling people en route. The psychological distance between the two is vast.

Whether life is lived in a big city or small town, transience and disjunction can create more clashing dissonance than enjoyable harmony. Competing commitments (work, immediate and extended family, friends past and present, dating relationships that come and go) and erratic tempos can make it difficult to have a consistent emotional engagement with the people around us and the tasks at hand. Juggling the variety of situations in which we find ourselves is challenging. In a woman's life, the prospects of marriage and motherhood loom as possibilities that would create even more radical changes.

When we understand all of life's relationships and the whole palette of our gifts—not just the ones we get paid for or that carry the official title of "wife" or "mother"—as our callings, themes begin to synthesize, and a sense of wholeness emerges among the many diverse pieces and stages of life.

"To see one's whole life as a divine 'calling' is…the cement which holds together the various aspects of our lives, preventing them from splitting up into different, and disjointed, sealed compartments," explains theologian Paul Helm. So in small-town Kansas, I'm the granddaughter, niece, and cousin I have always been, and that is as much a part of what God has called me to as my current employment.

Understanding Callings Helps Prepare Us for Season Changes in Life

A woman's life is like Chicago. From education to getting a job to marriage to motherhood to empty nest, the transitions involve significant changes—like the distinct seasons of the Windy City, where summer is hot, winter is brutal, spring rains can last forever, and fall finally provides a relative lull.

A man's life is more like Tampa (or maybe Anchorage, depending on your perspective)—little variation in the seasons, pretty consistent in terms of major expectations and duties. Traditionally, once a man completes formal education, he gets a job and keeps working for the next forty or even fifty years, day in and day out. Work generally remains a constant in a young man's outlook on the future.

In a woman's long view of life, however, work is typically a variable. A young working woman looking forward to marriage has to anticipate some major season changes, and that can create turmoil.

"I love my work, but it's fifty hours a week," says a female FBI agent. "The things I work on right now, I think about in the shower, in the car, they show up in my dreams... There is no way I could have a family life and work at what I do now with the same kind of hours.

"Every time I step into a relationship that looks like it has potential, I have all this angst. I start preparing myself to detach from professional life. Even if I remain a part-time professional, it would be completely different from what I do now. So I go through this battle where I try to envision myself pulling away from my current work life and moving toward family life.

"Then when the relationship ends, I have to do a reverse of all that. I've been through this process a few times. Sometimes, at the end, it's a relief that I don't have to work so hard on detaching myself."

That internal squall at the prospect of a major life transition is as inevitable as a tornado on the brink of season change in Chicago. The assurance of a consistent ultimate calling helps us keep our bearings no matter how erratic the seasons may be. If a false spring blooms, understanding our circumstances as a part of our callings prevents us from turning frigid toward life, toward men, toward God.

Callings Remind Us Who's in Charge

There is no "calling without a Caller," says Os Guinness, author of *The Call*. And we are accountable to the One who gives us our call.

But there are other voices too.

Well-meaning recruiters offer all manner of life and career counseling for free—some of it sought, some unsought, some welcome, some unwelcome. Inevitably, much of it is conflicting. One of my colleagues discourages almost every young person from going to law school, saying, "Too many go just because they have no other clear path." Another work associate, who is an anthropologist by training and *not* an attorney, says, "You can *always* use a law degree," reasoning that law school should always be the default option, *especially* if a young person isn't sure what to do.

Other advice emphasizes tradition, such as, "Your father and I met at Baylor, and it's where all your siblings have gone." Some are so enthusiastic about their path that they'd like to lend you their life script. Tempting as it might be to plagiarize, a life story can't be duplicated.

Seeking counsel is critical, and getting second opinions is a good thing. But soliciting advice about choices of life direction is different from taking a poll: you need more than a majority vote to decide the matter.

With all the competing messages from recruiters throughout life, knowing that we have an ultimate Boss to whom we will one day report face to face will keep us from being batted about by endless opinions and dueling schools of thought. Understanding life as a set of callings given by the One who calls keeps us focused on the One to whom we are accountable. We will always be pulled in multiple directions. Whose voice do we listen to?

Callings Keep Us Going

We don't take time off or retire from our callings. Being single doesn't mean we are living outside the purposes we were made for. God's call is the current that runs through all the seasons and phases of our lives. God's call folds the story of our lives into His kingdom narrative, and whatever our season of life, we should see our lives as serving His eternal purposes.

We are en route to a destination, and today is a travel day, during which we are growing closer to that goal. No matter how many false starts, backtracks, stalls, and breakdowns we encounter along the way, we can be sure of reaching the destination. Centuries ago, a preacher put it this way:

> We are not yet what we shall be, but we are growing toward it; the process is not yet finished, but it is going on; this is not the end, but it is the road; all does not yet gleam with glory, but all is being purified.

The lasting significance of today is the faithfulness with which we respond to our callings. Dealing with decisions in this unexpected in-between is the immediate challenge.

Eleven

How Will I Know? Making Sense of Choices in Single Life

Mr. Harper was notorious at my high school for crafting nettlesome multiple-choice exam questions in his world history class. "Choose the best answer," the instructions would read, and then the list of possible answers would extend through almost half the alphabet. Choices A through D were typically all plausible responses in their own right. But then he would throw in an assortment of additional options that would make our minds spin:

(e) all of the above

(f) a and c

(g) b and d

(h) a, b, and c

(i) none of the above

His exams became the bane of our existence as high-school underclassmen. But we did learn to be more discerning that year.

In the undefined time between college graduation and wedding day, choices seem to present themselves in similarly complex bundles. Very few options can immediately be tossed aside as wrong or irrelevant. Instead, decision making often seems like splitting hairs to try to determine the very best choice. The multiple choices in themselves can be daunting. Knowing the right criteria to use in making a judgment call among them may be the toughest part of all.

There is a way to get past feeling habitually confused or repeatedly incapacitated at decision-making crossroads. A Christian should be confident that she is living in God's will, that God has called her to the place where she is, and that He takes pleasure in what she does for His glory.

What's God's Will Got to Do with It?

A friend who worked in a job placement office reached a point of frustration with candidates who couldn't make up their minds. They would go through first and second interviews, entertain offers, and then turn apathetically indecisive.

The indecision was worse among the Christians than the non-Christians she dealt with. "They think that God is going to give them a direct sign, put the manna right in front of them with a note attached that says, 'Eat me!'" she explained.

We can tie ourselves in knots trying to tease out the will of God for our lives. Many decisions are complicated, and some leave us deeply conflicted. But we're not flying blind when it comes to the will of God. We just need to know what to look for.

Universals: *What God Has Made Clear in His Word*

God has made many things abundantly clear in His Word: tell the truth on your résumé, look after your family, don't sleep around, don't marry someone who doesn't share your faith in Christ, and lots of other instructions. These are the basic ground rules. They don't change. Everything else will, but not these.

What God has made clear in His Word has many implications for the way we live our lives. Some of the major guideposts are these:

- *Loving God.* "Love the Lord your God with all your heart and with all your soul and with all your strength and with all your mind" (Luke 10:27).
- *Loving others.* "Love your neighbor as yourself" (Luke 10:27).
- *Character qualities.* "But the fruit of the Spirit is love, joy, peace, patience, kindness, goodness, faithfulness, gentleness and self-control" (Galatians 5:22–23).
- *Self-control.* "Therefore, prepare your minds for action; be self-controlled; set your hope fully on the grace to be given you when Jesus Christ is revealed. As obedient children, do not conform to the evil desires you had when you lived in ignorance. But just as he who called you is holy, so be holy in all you do; for it is written: 'Be holy, because I am holy'" (1 Peter 1:13–16).

Local Conditions: *What God Has Made Clear in Your Situation*

Providence is not an ancient clockmaker who turned the crank long ago to set the world in motion and then left it to its own devices.

Nor is it a force that occasionally breaks in to change the course of world events. Providence is the continual work of a personal God intervening in our lives to guide and shape us, just as He guides and shapes all of creation.

Providence is the way God works out His purposes as Creator and Redeemer. As Creator, God not only made all things, but He continues to govern all things. As Redeemer, God ordains the circumstances that will accomplish His calling of a people to Himself.

To say that God is sovereign is to believe that He will accomplish His purposes, both as Creator and Redeemer. This means we are not victims of circumstance, nor are we at the mercy of those around us. We, and all our circumstances, are in the merciful hands of God.

If you believe that, then you can also have the assurance that where you are is where you are supposed to be. You have not been demoted to a consolation plan B if you are single, unemployed, or generally not where you thought you'd be at this point in life. Plan B does not exist.

Everything about our situations—from the way each of us is made, physically and psychologically, to the experiences we've had, to the family we've come from—is a part of God's design. These everyday conditions and ordinary capacities form the context in which we are to accomplish the lofty goals of glorifying God and loving our neighbor.

That makes today less about what is happening to us and more about what we are doing with today—and, more important, what God is doing with today. This day's events, expected or not, are a part of God's callings for us and of God's purposes for His kingdom. How we respond is what matters.

More often than not, our most mundane and unglamorous callings—such as loving the people we live with—are the most challenging. As Alyosha of the quarreling Karamazovs reminds his brother Ivan, "It may be conceivable to love one's fellow man at a distance, but it is almost never possible to love him at close quarters."

Still, the everyday struggles that try us most are the truest test of our faithfulness to our first call. As Martin Luther said:

> If I profess with the loudest voice and clearest exposition
> every portion of the Word of God except precisely that little
> point which the world and the devil are at that moment
> attacking, I am not confessing Christ, however boldly I may
> be professing Him. Where the battle rages there the loyalty of
> the soldier is proved; and to be steady on all the battle front
> besides, is mere flight and disgrace if he flinches at that point.

What Have You Been Given?

Our callings are entrusted to us, and we are accountable to God for the way that we live them out. Each role and relationship we find ourselves in, by birth (daughter, sister) or by station in life (student, employee, neighbor), carries certain responsibilities to others. Our relationship to Christ gives us a role within His eternal kingdom that should shape our perspective on all other relationships and responsibilities in life. The talents we're born with are gifts of God to be used for His glory and the good of others, and we will give account for how we use them through life. Likewise, life changes—whether coming into money or getting cleaned out by a hurricane—and opportunities that present themselves are a part of our callings; God is interested in what we make of them.

A story Jesus told illustrates how we are to be accountable for what He has entrusted to us. A rich man going on a journey gives a sizable sum of money to several of his servants. "'Put this money to work,' he said, 'until I come back'" (Luke 19:13). When he returns, the first two servants report that they have earned substantial increases above the original sum. The boss is impressed, and he gives them more responsibility. But a third servant returns only what he had initially been given. It turns out he had hidden it in a piece of cloth while the boss was away. He tries to rationalize this lack of initiative, but the boss doesn't want to hear about it. He reprimands the servant for neglecting the charge he had given him: to put the money to work.

In modern terms, stewarding what has been given to us means that we think of life like a portfolio of callings that we are to manage, ultimately returning it to God as the response to our first call. All our relationships, gifts, challenges, and opportunities are parts of our personal callings. Hearing, "Well done, good and faithful servant," will be the crowning achievement of a life spent responding to His call.

God has created us with gifts, and we are obligated to discover,

develop, and pursue our giftedness as circumstances and responsibilities permit. To leave those gifts latent or neglected because we
were too busy looking out for marriage is dereliction of duty.

What Do You Like?

Being in a job that doesn't fit could be compared to trying to walk
ten steps in shoes that make you wince. Clearly, buying those
shoes was a mistake, however attractive they might have appeared.
A job fits when it suits our inclinations and interests. These inner
leanings are a naturally occurring set of cues to tip us off to our
callings.

Desires also well up within us in the decision-making process.
But desires can represent mixed motives: some direct us in ways that
will please God, others in ways that won't. Sorting through them
requires discernment.

When we train our desires to be like the Lord's, the desires of our
heart are trustworthy indicators that help us to determine God's guidance in our lives. "Delight yourself in the LORD and he will give you
the desires of your heart," says Psalm 37:4. If we believe that God's
will is to bring about our eternal good, then we have every reason to
pray for our desires to be more and more like God's desires for us.

What Are You Like?

When a woman who had worked in the midst of third-world poverty
and hardship returned to the States, working in an air-conditioned

downtown office stressed her out. Stressors come in all varieties, but the capacity for handling stress isn't one-size-fits-all. All kinds of conditions can fray nerves, from stabilizing a patient's falling blood pressure to organizing a high-dollar fund-raiser or facing a class of hyperactive fifth graders. Some people would take a medical emergency over an elementary school classroom any day.

One person's stress can be another person's source of satisfaction. The capacities and gifts we've been given as individuals make all the difference. When passion, gifts, and opportunity coincide, it stirs a deep sense of satisfaction: *I was made for this.* Meanwhile, knowing we are participating in a purpose greater than ourselves gives us an "I can change the world" rush.

One of the all-time best descriptions of this awestruck sense of purpose comes from the film *Chariots of Fire,* the story of the Olympic runner Eric Liddell. In one scene, his sister tries to persuade him to join her in mission work in China. But he resists, explaining that he feels compelled to race rather than to go abroad at that time: "[God] made me fast, and when I run I feel His pleasure.... To give it up would be to hold Him in contempt. But to run and win is to honor Him."

Eric Liddell sensed that his calling was to glorify God through running because God had made him *fast.* Others God has made savvy, strong, technical, patient, or compassionate. These gifts point us toward the unique callings God has for each of us.

God the Creator custom-fits His people for their tasks. He equips us with the capacity to accomplish what He's called us to do. That means He has sized and tailored our gifts appropriately to our tasks.

Generally, we should seek opportunities that will fit us: neither too far beyond our capacity, leaving us frustrated by falling short; nor too small, stifling us or letting our abilities atrophy. The appropriate level of challenge should engage our interests and gifts while giving us opportunity to grow. Judging the ideal fit is similar to how we would be sized for shoes as a child; the salesclerk would ask whether there was room to wiggle our toes to make sure we wouldn't grow out of the new shoes too quickly.

We should aim where our inclination and ability overlap, writes Arthur F. Miller Jr., author of *Why You Can't Be Anything You Want to Be.* (Sure, you might *want* to sing like an *American Idol* champion, but if you're tone deaf, you probably aren't being directed to sing.) Being *anything* won't satisfy you. Instead, states Miller, "You'll love being who you were designed to be."

Identifying inclinations and gifts takes effort. It requires time for stillness, solitude, reflection, and prayer. It involves taking inventory of what you're like and what you like to do. It also demands vulnerability, such as asking friends and family for feedback about what you're good at and what you're not so good at. That's especially important for singles who may not be in a living situation that has an automatic feedback loop.

When it comes to negative feedback, we tend to get quite comfortable criticizing those closest to us. As singles, however, it's possible to retreat from most relationships that cause us discomfort and to surround ourselves with people who tell us what we like to hear. But if we're to make progress in life, it's a good idea to make sure we regularly get some straight talk.

This kind of self-assessment calls for sober judgment (as Romans 12:3 counsels) so we don't over- or underestimate ourselves. Pride is a well-known stumbling block. But false modesty and perpetual self-doubt can also prevent us from using our gifts to the fullest and so make us poor stewards of our callings.

As much as possible, our external lives should mirror our inner lives. What we do should be as close a match as we can find for what we're like and what we like to do. Most important, *how* we do what we do should reflect our first call.

Getting Over Gambling on the Prospect of Marriage

For any young woman who has grown up wanting to be married, it is tempting to treat marriage like plan A for life and singleness like a plan B alternative, a second-rate status. Meg was an exception. She had another way of looking at plan A and plan B.

While in her twenties, Meg had decided to leave her job for law school, and two months after signing on the dotted line, she started dating someone. It grew serious enough that she had second thoughts about starting school that fall.

But she decided to go ahead with law school and explained her decision to her roommate Carli: "I am single today—that's where God has me, so that is plan A. While I am single, I want to pursue fully what God has put before me, and right now, that's law school. If God would have me marry, then that is up to His purposes and

His timing. If and when He moves me into that plan B, I'll trust Him to take care of what that means for plan A."

Singleness was plan A, because it was reality at the moment. Marriage was plan B, because it didn't exist yet as a true option. Marriage would become a real option when she got engaged, and that would be the time to consider what changes would need to be made in education and work because of her commitment to marry. As it turned out, after her first year of law school, Meg did marry the man she was dating. She transferred schools, completed a second year, had a baby, took a year off, completed a third year to graduate, and had a second baby. Now she's pregnant with their third.

For a single woman, thinking through the implications of educational and career decisions is critical. It is important to recognize the potential for future trade-offs and sacrifices of personal plans that were made before the commitment of marriage. But living with one foot in the reality of plan A and the other in the hypothetical plan B is not much of a plan for anything but frustration and discontentment.

"I think of Meg's plan A versus plan B every time I come to a decision-making juncture in education and career," said Carli, now thirty and a college professor. "I am open to marriage, and I would be excited to share my life with someone and to have a family someday. But that someday is not today. I have learned that the best way to be fulfilled in Christ is to give my all to what He has for me today. And today, that is singleness, so I will run hard after Him for all that means in my life—family, friends, church involvement, and education and work goals."

The Fine Print

Even as we seek to make the most of what God has given us, there is no guarantee that we'll always be able to use our gifts to their full capacity. The calling equation is made up of a shifting balance of relationships, responsibilities, gifts, and opportunities. Sometimes life's demands require taking a job that's less satisfying than the ideal, such as working retail to pay off college loans when you'd rather be painting watercolors. Sometimes duty to family calls, trumping other desires. But even when we're off of our preferred route, we're still squarely within our callings.

Nor is there any guarantee that our callings will all be pleasant. "I've become immune to the platitudes, like 'God will take care of you,'" said one woman. "He does provide, but it's not always God's will for us to have a pleasant life." She's very aware, even in her darkest moments, that her life is full of blessings.

The purpose of our journey is to bring glory to God by becoming more like Him. He uses our situations, including hardship and struggle, to make that happen.

Joseph of Old Testament fame clearly had talent, but his potential kept being thwarted, and his path was anything but pleasant. Twice in his life, major sabotages at the hands of those closest to him sent him into some of the worst imaginable conditions—sold into slavery by his own brothers and then framed by his boss's wife for a sexual act he refused to commit. He had worked his way up from slave trade victim to head steward for a prominent Egyptian named Potiphar, only to be thrown into jail on the basis of a false accusation.

The anguish Joseph must have felt when he was handed over to slave-trading merchants, and later when the prison doors locked behind him, could easily have taken root in bitterness and grown into revenge. Yet when Joseph's gifts came to the attention of his fellow inmates, and eventually to the attention of the most powerful person in all Egypt, he used his prominence to bring blessing on the very ones who had done him such harm. Joseph's counsel to Pharaoh saved the Egyptians as well as his own family from the famine that soon came upon the land.

And with grace that could have come only from one who knows he has received grace, Joseph forgave his double-crossing brothers and assured them of his conviction that all he had gone through was part of his calling from God. "You intended to harm me, but God intended it for good to accomplish what is now being done, the saving of many lives" (Genesis 50:20).

Wrongful imprisonment is, thankfully, a prospect few of us have to fear. But betrayal, bitter disappointment, loss, and aching loneliness are not so rare. In pursuing our callings, we shouldn't be surprised to encounter hardship or think that we are outside God's will because a stroke of sadness crosses our path. When the desires of our hearts prove elusive, we must know that something larger is at work for purposes that we may not see.

Last year a friend left a successful job and a social life she enjoyed to move home, two thousand miles away, to be with her family as her father struggled with terminal cancer. Looking back on the year, she is frank: "It hasn't been fun, and it hasn't been happy. But some things are more important than happiness," she explained. "And I have a deep sense of joy that I am where I'm supposed to be."

PART 5

Living Right Now

Twelve

Mirroring the Image of God

The night train leaving Venice was crowded with summer vaca-
tioners. As college-age travelers, we were saving the cost of a hostel
by traveling at night. Since we couldn't afford sleeper bunks or
reserved seats, we jostled past each other in the unreserved cars,
bumping backpacks in the narrow hallway as we peered into sliding-
door cabins in search of an empty space. In many of them, sleeping
passengers sprawled across more than their share of the six places on
two facing benches, but waking them to insinuate oneself into the
cramped and stuffy quarters would only make everyone more
uncomfortable.

I was weary of searching car to car for an opening, so I decided
to stand until a few passengers might peel off at a stop down the line.
I found a quieter car with less through-traffic and propped myself
against the window with my bag at my feet.

The rhythm of the train's motion reached a lulling hum that
hushed the commotion among the Venetian boarders, who gradually
sifted into the cracks of one cabin or another. As the train left the

range of the city's lights, the interior scene sank into the surrounding half-light.

Idyllic moments have a way of creeping up unannounced, and this was one of them. The dark blue sky had soothed all the surroundings but for a bright moon that made the waterways dance as we skimmed their surface, with the mellow evening air streaming by the open window as their accompaniment. It was as exquisite as some of the art and architecture we had come to see.

Ten years later I had a similar sensation while driving home from work on a placid fall evening, listening to the mellifluous voice of Norah Jones. Rolling to a stop on a tree-lined suburban street, everything was still and soothing. The air seemed to have neither motion nor temperature of its own as it faded onto my arm that was resting out the window. I hadn't expected to encounter such tranquillity on an average Tuesday in September.

Much of the journeying between those two points was spent inching home in a rush-hour traffic jam or driving sixty miles an hour for a weekend away—struggling to get to a better situation and not really enjoying the ride. Even the destination often failed to live up to expectations.

We spend much of our lives pursuing the idyllic conditions of a summer night near Venice or a fall afternoon filled with velvet air and soothing voices. Naturally occurring moments of pure contentment are few and fleeting, however. We're more likely to stumble onto them than to contrive them.

Circumstantial contentment is an unsure destination that eludes us and satisfies little beyond a few memories of golden moments. Aiming for just-right conditions will keep us striving for situations that may disappoint our expectations or may never materialize at all. The very things we imagine will bring contentment may bring us new and different sorts of challenges and frustrations, whether a fabulous new job, a dream house, or a dream spouse. We may have visions of wedded bliss, but as any married couple will tell you, the reality is decidedly mixed—the result of human sinfulness.

The better way is a model that the apostle Paul preached and lived: "I have learned the secret of being content in any and every situation, whether well fed or hungry, whether living in plenty or in want" (Philippians 4:12).

Paul's secret—and the one that Hilary, Emma, Carli, and others have caught on to—is the satisfaction of bringing glory to God through obedience in our callings. If joy springs from what is within us rather than what is around us, we can find it here and now as well as in the not yet—even as we await the ultimate heavenly completion of our contentment in Christ. Finding that secret of contentment for the present begins with some concrete decisions about our relationship with God and with others.

Tending the Spirit Within

God made human beings, alone among all living creatures, in His image. We can cultivate the image of God within by practicing spiritual disciplines and guarding our hearts and minds.

Practice Spiritual Disciplines

Growing to be more like Christ is the most important part of life in all seasons. We grow in this way by reading God's Word, praying, and being joined to His church.

These spiritual disciplines are for us here and now. Today—not the next season of life—is the time to develop the habits of spiritual discipline. It's tempting to think that it will be easier to find time to read the Bible or pray more consistently after the next deadline or milestone.

After I get done with graduate school...

After my busy season at work...

Once I settle down and get married...

We need the benefit of spiritual discipline as much today as we do after that next milestone—and for whatever lies unknown in-between.

Guard Heart and Mind

Most of us are prone to anxious thoughts and worry. Our minds are tempted to go down all kinds of rabbit trails imagining worst-case scenarios. Stopping worry is almost a physical task. We can't just repress it; we have to pull it out like a weed and replace it with something more edifying, or it will grow right back.

Guarding our thoughts is a habit that at times is not merely a daily duty. It can be an hour-by-hour or minute-by-minute task, a direct struggle between rebel thoughts and those things that Scripture explicitly tells us to think about: "Whatever is true, whatever is noble, whatever is right, whatever is pure, whatever is lovely, whatever is admirable…excellent or praiseworthy" (Philippians 4:8). We must actively choose to think on these things and to ask for God's help to do so.

Sometimes our circumstances prompt us to ask God why, and sometimes He leads us to a gracious plateau where we can see the purpose in the broken path. At other times there may be parts we can't figure out, turns that our lives have taken that don't make sense for a long, long time or perhaps ever in this lifetime. These become the mind's Sit 'N Spin.

Remember the Sit 'N Spin? It's a merry-go-round for one, a simple plastic disk a child sits on cross-legged around a short stem in the center on which a sort of steering wheel is mounted. By working that wheel hand over hand, a child can get the disk—and herself—spinning, and soon it has a momentum all its own and just keeps her spinning until she's too dizzy to see straight.

Watching the world whirl by is a fun pastime for a child, but as an adult, it's far from enjoyable to have that going on inside. Just like the child on a Sit 'N Spin, the mind churns obsessively on things we cannot understand, like why someone else got that dream job or why that relationship ended so abruptly or why so-and-so never called again.

Wrestling with such perplexities is necessary, and the more severe the pain or misunderstanding, the longer the wrestling will take. But when such obsessive patterns of thought become a distraction from the things we are called to in Christ, that's when we have to pray to leave them behind, even without understanding fully at that point.

Bitterness is a choice. One way to avoid it is to choose not to engage in cynical conversation. One woman in her early forties told me she has decided not to spend lots of time with single women who resent their singleness. She's deliberate about pursuing contentment. "When I grow old, I want to be the woman who is known for her prayers and her sweet spirit, not a bitter old lady. It's about surrender, and seeking to be like Christ."

Lisa, thirty-nine, describes two big decision points in her life: The first, at age twenty-five, was to do something with her life other than wait around in a dead-end job to get married—as she saw some women in their later twenties doing. The second came at around age thirty after a tough breakup, when she made the conscious choice to be happy with or without a man.

"It's about balance and not allowing one variable to dominate. If you're single, it's not allowing the missing variable to dominate; if you're married, it means not allowing marriage to dominate as the be-all-end-all," she says.

Pursuing the Fullness of Truth, Beauty, and Goodness

Our nature reflects the image of God in many ways, and we should seek to mirror Him in all of them. In addition to our spiritual characteristics, another way in which we reflect the likeness of the Creator is in our creative capacity. Human beings can design, produce, form, and craft in a vast array of fields. We also have the ability to recognize excellence and beauty, to cultivate it, and to appreciate it.

When we spend a majority of our waking hours at work, it's easy to neglect certain other aspects of our nature. We need to find equilibrium between professional and domestic pursuits. We need to engage in nurturing and creative expression as well as critical thinking.

Cultivate a Sense of Appreciation

One of the ways we reflect God's image is in our appreciation of beauty and goodness. God said that creation was good. We can echo Him in that assessment; other creatures don't have that capacity. While we drive west on I-80 admiring the setting sun, a cow we pass in a roadside pasture may be benefiting from its heat, but the cow is not meditating on the exquisite hues of red and orange. A horizon on fire *does* spark something in a human heart, however, and that spark ought to ignite praise to God.

But if we're too busy thinking about how fast we can get to our destination, we're likely to miss the sunset.

God called His creation good, and His creation includes our senses and our ability to appreciate the goodness and beauty around us. Following the pattern of God's pronouncement that His work was good, we also have a duty to know the good, to love the good, and to call others to love the good as well. Unlike God, however, we have to work at recognizing, knowing, and loving what is good, because that's not always our natural tendency. To cultivate this aspect of the image of God within us, we need to take time to nurture our sense of appreciation, developing our senses to perceive

SHE SAYS: ADVICE FOR TWENTYSOMETHING WOMEN

Understand that there are no deadlines on your life. Put your expectations aside. Have goals and visions for yourself, but if you think, *I have to achieve such and such or else,* you're setting yourself up for disappointment. Don't spend your life thinking, *When I am...*   —Sharon, 29

God is creative, and He has an individual purpose for you. You are uniquely made to accomplish things on earth, and His timing is different for everyone.   —Carrie, 44

Find some good Christian women mentors, personally and professionally. Married or single, as long as they're balanced in most areas of life, learn from their life choices.   —Tricia, 41

When it comes to choices about what you're going to do in terms of education or work or a move...one of the most valuable lessons I've learned is that you can always change your mind.   —Joy, 34

Guard your heart. Every single relationship shapes you. Be wise about your choices.   —Jen, 30

Don't waste a minute of your time waiting around; use every moment to have good relationships with your friends and serve the Lord in every way you can. We're single and free; use that to your advantage. Then you won't have to look back and realize you wasted all this time.   —Ann, 34

Find a community and commit.   —Kimberly, 28

Be committed. Too often our pattern is to go in, get what we need, and get out—whether it's a church, an outside group, or a relationship.   —Lynn, 37

In my twenties I felt really torn up about not meeting the love of my life; now I don't feel that way. Instead of carrying that around on your shoulders like Atlas, set it aside, don't lose sight of it altogether; it's there, but it doesn't have to overwhelm you.   —Lisa, 39

Don't be surprised if your twenties turn out to be tough. You're going to have to deal with job, finances, finding a place to live, etc. It's not all fun and games. There will be failures and disappointments. But if you're expecting that, you can take it in stride.   —Ellie, 29 what is beautiful to the eye, to the ear, and to the touch, taste, and smell.

"Taste and see that the LORD is good," the Scriptures say (Psalm 34:8). We should appreciate God and His goodness in creation with more than our minds. God has created this world with intricacy and artistry that are beyond our capacity to comprehend; all our pursuits will barely scratch the surface. To know this world is to praise God for His creation.

Ultimately, this is why we learn. This is why we should know about the world God created, the works of His hands and the works of His creatures. Innate curiosity and competitive spirit as a motivation for learning only get a person so far. Reading great works of literature, discovering poetry, and listening to the best composers are all ways that we learn to love the Creator more. As we appreciate these things, we appreciate more of what He has done.

That applies not only to the natural world but also to culture and society. Our creative capacity should serve others. This, in part, is how we redeem the time between life's milestones. Life is more than merely marking time with big celebrations like a graduation or a wedding. It is also all that goes on in-between those milestones.

This is why we garden or spend three hours to prepare a meal or get up early to the see the sunrise. These are ways that we enjoy God's creation and, therefore, ways we enjoy God Himself.

This is how we truly do all things to the glory of God, which gives meaning to the seemingly mundane. Enjoying God's creation makes our daily lives become more than going through the motions, more than drudgery, more than keeping up with the next-door neighbor. Tending to the details of this moment prevents the now from being swallowed up in longing for the not yet.

Enjoy the Here and Now

In France, my roommate and I shared an apartment that faced the building where our married friends Thomas and Maggie lived. Their patio was close enough to our window to carry on a conversation across the narrow alley. Thomas was the head of the school, and Maggie coordinated the elementary-school program.

It had been a busy and demanding year, and things got even more hectic as spring arrived. Thomas and Maggie were planning a move back to the States in June, and she was pregnant and miserable with morning sickness. Each day became a struggle of staying even-keeled enough to carry on at school, to maintain some order at home, and to prepare for the move while trying to get a little rest.

One day in May when the weather finally started getting warmer, we noticed Thomas planting red geraniums in window boxes for their patio. With all the schoolwork, housework, packing, and caring for his sick wife, why would he bother to plant flowers? He and Maggie would only be in the apartment a few more weeks, and it didn't seem worth it. How could they even enjoy geraniums at a time like this?

Most of us heading home at the end of the school year had thrown aesthetics out the window weeks before and were finishing out our year with just the bare necessities. For Thomas, however, this moment was as much worthy of enjoyment as his first days in France two years earlier. Since he had set foot in the country, he had been intentional about appreciating the way of life around him and was ever curious about the culture and history of this particular corner in the fabric of God's creation. Planting geraniums might not have resulted from a conscious theological rationale at the time, but his deep convictions that God has called us to enjoy His creation and that we should make the most of each moment had simply become a way of life.

Thirteen

Choosing Community

Single freedom lets us lead autonomous lives. As singles, we can treat most of our relationships as disposable. When a relationship has served our purposes, we can leave it behind. We have few, if any, contractual relationships that bind us in commitment to others, and that makes it much easier to walk away whenever we feel like it. Family is an exception, but even with them we can maintain distance by moving halfway across the country or even around the world.

This phase of life can easily be consumed by professional demands and shallow social interactions. Denying or downplaying the depth of our relational nature can breed a sense of detachment. But even as singles, we need to be in committed relationships to which we are accountable and can give and receive love.

Commitment is a good habit to practice if we hope one day to be married. "I can imagine that it will be challenging for me to be in a relationship for the rest of my life because I've had almost forty years of moving on to something else. I haven't been living in a way that has trained or prepared me for that," said a woman in Washington DC. Relationships force us to deal with our selfishness, as another woman in her early forties observed, "Being single for so long, I'm aware that I can be selfish in certain ways. My girlfriends and I sometimes criticize guys for that, but I'm realizing, *Well, so am I.*"

Join a Church Congregation

Committing to a church congregation and becoming a member is a practical, but critical, step for growing in grace and living out our first call to Christ. By responding to that call, we have entered a covenant with God, and we should reflect that covenant in our commitment to the body of Christ here on earth.

It's tempting not to commit seriously and consistently to a church congregation. Sleeping in on Sundays, keeping weekend options open, or church-hopping in search of the perfect congregation can keep us from committing to a regular time and place to worship the Lord with fellow believers.

The transience of single life can be another excuse. But the lack of permanence shouldn't become a pretext for failing to commit to a congregation. Some military families are a great example in this regard. Because they're frequently relocating—typically every three years or so—it would be easy for them not to get involved with a local church in each new post. But these families are sometimes the most invested in the life of the congregation; they know better than those of us who have stayed in one place a long time how important it is to have fellowship, even when their stay is likely to be short.

"It's tempting to avoid accountability as a single," said forty-two-year-old Rachel, who lives in a small community in Virginia.

"I'm a part of a small church body, and I do have accountability there. If I'm not at church on Sunday, I get three phone calls to make sure I'm okay!"

When looking for a church, seek out a local congregation that provides solid preaching from the Bible that will challenge you to grow in Christ. Find a community that functions as the body of Christ, where the Great Commission is taken seriously, where opportunities are available to use your gifts for the kingdom of God, where members know one another and bear one another's burdens, where they hold one another accountable to a life of holiness and growing in grace.

Look for a church that, in its preaching and programs, encourages all its members to pursue individual sanctification in their current situation, regardless of age or marital status. The church should communicate that it is valuable to have interaction across generations and life situations, since all of us together make up the body of Christ.

Find a place where people from different perspectives in life interact and share a common life together as a community of believers. It should be a place where you are closely connected to the congregation as a whole or to a circle of believing friends, a place where your presence is welcomed and from which your absence would be felt.

Keep Close Friends for Life

As geographically mobile as singles can be, it's tough to maintain consistency in friendships. It's a wise investment to make a close friend or two early in life and keep her close as long as you can, ideally for as long as you both live. That friend should be someone who will tell you when you're wrong or that she's worried about you, someone who can affirm that you're headed the right way when you're not sure, someone who won't be afraid to ask you what you did last night. That friend should be someone who will make time to laugh, cry, or pray with you on the phone, whether you live down the street or seven time zones away. Maintaining such a lifelong friendship means making it a priority to commit time regularly to visit, call, or communicate in some way.

Keep Diverse Company

Look for opportunities to spend time with people in different life situations. At times it helps to be with people who identify with your experiences and struggles. Pregnant women swap stories, and old ladies talk about how times have changed, and that's one way of bearing one another's burdens.

But to spend all our time focused on problems like our own can give us the false impression that burdens come in one shape and size and can cause us to lose a sense of proportion in life. Our peers sitting in the same situation tend to share our blind spots. Being with those in different life stages and struggles puts our own heartaches and hardships in perspective.

"It has made a huge difference in my life to be involved with families," said Rachel, forty-two. "Not just involvement on a surface level, but really being good friends with people who aren't young married couples. You contribute to their family, and they give a lot back. You see what the real life of marriage is all about, and it keeps you grounded. It's not this ideal pie in the sky. It's hard work."

Make Heart-Wise Housing Choices

Figuring out whether to rent or to buy is a major decision when it comes to housing. But whether to live alone or with roommates is an equally significant decision, and spiritual and emotional needs should be serious considerations in that choice. Seasons of struggle with anxiety or depression, for example, may not be good times to live alone.

"Years ago I was dating a great guy I was sure I would marry, so I purposely was renting and living alone. We dated three years, got engaged, but broke it off soon after. After the breakup, some friends said they didn't think it was a good idea to continue living alone, to help avoid self-centeredness," said Tricia, forty-one.

"I'm very independent, and I like living alone, but I did move in with some roommates for several years after that, and I think it was a good decision and good for me during that time." She continued, "Now I own my own place and live alone again, so we'll see what happens."

Fourteen

Honorable Intentions

It's seven in the morning on a Wednesday, and my sister is singing along melodramatically to REO Speedwagon while she puts on her makeup. Then, leaning her head out the bathroom door, she bursts out over the music, "That's what I love about eighties music—it's so passionate! It just takes your heart and stomps on it!" She illustrates with her makeup brush as though she is pulverizing a piece of meat.

Three-year-old Catherine, the daughter of some friends, is attracted to a different version of the same sentiment. She loves the movie *Black Beauty.* She's fascinated by horses and intrigued by the story, but she also loves getting her heartstrings pulled. Before the film is over, she always ends up quietly weeping. Her dad, Jerry, has a hard time understanding this aspect of female nature. Why would she want to watch something that she knows will cause her emotional pain?

A Check on Emotions

The female mind can spin a romantic comedy out of the most mea-
ger material from male interaction, then rewrite it as a tragic tale of
love lost—in the space of a few waiting hours or days. After an
anguishing week or two, the mind can spin a whole tale about why
he hasn't been in touch. Meanwhile, serial romances that end in bitterness or frustration can create further angst.

An unsatisfied heart is prone to tantrums and obsessive thinking. Obsessive thoughts about the unknown don't go away meekly;
we must actively counter these thoughts by engaging the mind elsewhere, and the best option is to contemplate the fact that God has
everything under control. Fretting is not a mark of trusting; we must
actively choose to trust God with our relationships. Emotions are
part of our nature, but they shouldn't tyrannically hold sway over
our lives.

The "need to know" what others are thinking about us is particularly troubling. It is unsettling to be unsure that we are in good
standing with someone whose opinion we care about. Our reaction
is often to grasp for some assurances of affection. That can become
an internal fixation and an external tendency to be clingy and suf-
focating in our interactions. To overcome this, we need selfless,
trusting, other-centered love to be stronger than fear in our
thoughts and actions.

A disciplined mind and heart governed by Christ should direct
our thoughts and passions so that they further our ability to enjoy

and glorify God. As John Piper wrote, "Christ…is the hard, immovable, unshapable, intractable Reality that banks the sea of emotion into a river that has to flow this way and not that, deep and not shallow."

Commit to Purity

Sexual purity is one of the ways we're called to reflect God's holiness. It's a prescription for our spiritual, physical, and emotional well-being.

Reasons for purity don't change with age, even if our feelings and urges do. "In your twenties you can say it's hard, but it's going to be over soon. But in your thirties you realize, *This may not end… Am I going to be celibate forever?* This is what's even harder than not having the white picket fence," said Lisa, thirty-nine.

Justifications for cutting corners are tempting. "I have some girlfriends my age who have become bitter because they wanted to be married, they prayed about it, and this is not what they asked for. So they justify their actions within relationships by saying, 'Well, I'm thirty-four years old; what am I supposed to do?'" says Ann, thirty-four.

Every young woman must make sexual purity a personal priority early and commit to it for all her single life. As an independent adult, it's not as simple as adopting someone else's list of dos and don'ts. It means having strong convictions anchored in a relationship with God in order to have the willpower to apply them when needed.

Men: Co-Heirs of the Kingdom, Co-Victims of the Chaos

Our Christian brothers are our co-heirs of the kingdom as well as co-victims of the chaos after feminism, the sexual revolution, and all the other changes of the last several decades. We all are confused, carry baggage, and make missteps. That calls for a charitable spirit toward one another. Rather than living by formulas that rely on coy manipulation or power games, we should seek to serve and encourage one another as we pursue our respective callings.

Women today have the freedom to take the initiative in building relationships with men, and sometimes those relationships have the potential to take a romantic turn. That leaves some women struggling with whether and how to use those opportunities. "Things have changed. How do you balance God's intervention with your own initiative, and what's godly? How much are we supposed to be doing about it?" wondered a thirty-year-old woman.

Choose Authenticity, Not Manipulation

"I tend to be someone who's kind of passive; in general, I let life come to me," said Candi. "My friend Julie is the opposite; she is very proactive. She did eHarmony, and she would make it known to all of our guy friends. I would tell her, *'Oh, Julie, calm down, you're going to scare people away!'* She didn't care. *'God's going to use all my deliberateness,'* she would tell me, and sure enough, He did. She met Ben, and they are so well suited for each other in so many ways, it's bizarre. They've been married for a year.

"She made me try it, and reluctantly I did—from July to September. I went on two dates with two different people. But I decided that's not for me. The way I connect with others is just a little more organic.

"God works within our personalities. I don't think online dating is for me, but it was for Julie. I don't think there's one godly way," Candi concluded.

Relationships are inextricably set in social and cultural contexts whose features are constantly changing. Christians seeking to apply biblical principles to those cultural contexts have espoused different philosophies and prescriptions for how to handle romance—even among those who agree that men and women are created different and that men should take the lead in relationships. "There are all these different techniques out there in the Christian world for pursuing relationships—something new every year it seems. They've all morphed together so much that I can't tell which is which. I don't think there's one particular formula that works. Just prayer!" said David, thirty-six.

"You've got to have a sense of the individual woman," said one man, suggesting that respect and sensitivity toward an individual woman's personality should steer a man's pursuit of her.

While there is no single immutable or biblical formula for launching romantic relationships, we do have clear guidance on how we should conduct ourselves in any relationship. We can't control the outcome of a relationship, but we are responsible for being faithful to our first call throughout its duration.

Honor Him

In any relationship with fellow believers, our objective is to appreciate one another as children of God, uniquely made in His image to glorify Him. We glorify God by honoring and enjoying one another, by reflecting His love to each other, and by helping one another pursue our callings. We do so within the context of our personalities, with our particular gifts and in the opportunities that present themselves—that is, within the context of our callings. We should seek to serve our communities according to how God has made us individually and in ways that will bring glory to Him.

This sense of purpose should define our behavior, whether in friendships or in romantic relationships. Sharing the love of Christ is a far different objective than merely snagging a man, and it will shape the way we interact with men. When our guiding purpose in a relationship is to delight in and respect the other person in a way that reflects how we enjoy and honor God, it will help to distinguish between manipulation and mind games on the one hand and purposeful investment on the other.

In all relationships we are called to love as we want to be loved and to exhibit the fruit of the Spirit: love, joy, peace, patience, kindness, goodness, faithfulness, gentleness, and self-control. If this is our outlook, we will want the best for the other person and not merely the gratification of our own desires.

Our lives should be a beautiful fragrance—"the aroma of Christ" (2 Corinthians 2:15). Like a perfume that lingers in a hall, we should aim for all of our interactions to leave others desiring what is good and right and true.

Fifteen

Marking Progress

A lot has changed for women since those of us in Generation X were born. We played more sports, pursued more advanced education, and have more job options than our mothers' generation. One thing that remains the same, however, is that almost all of us still want to be married and have children.

Our desire and expectation for marriage may not be new, but our reality is. Marriage proposals don't seem to coincide with college diplomas as frequently as they did in the past. In today's postgraduation working world, the obstacles to lasting love seem to loom larger, and romantic progress often lags behind career advancement.

Cultural confusion about male-female relationships in general, and marriage in particular, has made this interior struggle all the more challenging. We may want marriage as much as our mothers did, but this is not our mothers' dating world.

Stranded in this unexpected in-between, it's tempting to get impatient with God, as though He were a concierge or travel guide who gave us bad directions. That sense of disorientation can sometimes cloud our judgment about where we should be headed for the time being. Choices about jobs, grad school, or living arrangements can lead to guessing and gambling about how a situation will suit our marital prospects. Emma, for example, chose not to go to med school in part because she thought it would hurt her prospects of marrying. What's more, others may read our personal choices as statements we don't intend. Carli decided to go to law school despite some others' negativity, not because she didn't want to marry, but because she thought it was the best use of her God-given gifts and interests.

In the gap between life here and life hoped for, the challenge is to live in the present, deliberately and contentedly, even as we desire something more for the future. That requires focus and a sense of purpose that won't be swayed by a fear of the future or a fear of what others will think. Ultimately, that single-mindedness comes from God's call.

Our first call is to glorify and enjoy God. That gives us a sense of identity, belonging, direction, and purpose. We glorify God through our personal callings—the relationships, responsibilities, gifts, and opportunities God has placed in our lives. Life's changing circumstances will present many ways in which we are to pursue that first call, and for now, that includes singleness.

God's plans for us as women are not one-size-fits-all. He calls us individually and leads each one of us on a custom-built track. God is creative when it comes to making us more like Himself—He's not limited by any of our expectations, including those about when, how, or whom we would marry. Instead, He uses all kinds of situations and conditions to mold us into His image.

Understanding all of life as a set of callings from God helps us live happily in the midst of today's circumstances. If what pleases God shapes our sense of pleasure, then nothing is more satisfying than to serve God and others with our gifts. The best thing for each of us right now is to live in obedience and joy where He currently has us.

Even if we don't have a clue about marriage at the moment, we can be confident in the choices we make right now. A Christian woman's confidence comes from knowing that God has called her to the place where she is, has equipped her for it, and takes pleasure in what she does for His glory.

God has created us with gifts, and we should discover, develop, and pursue our areas of giftedness as our circumstances and other responsibilities permit. Focusing too much on marriage may cause us to leave those gifts undeveloped or overlooked. Marriage may be a part of our callings at some point, but for the moment, there are others at hand. To view each role in our lives as a calling from God is to understand that He has invested significance in it. That means we haven't missed the mark if we're not married. Singleness, too, is a part of His design.

How do we make sense of life now as we look forward to the not yet? Taking cues from women who have been down the road of singleness for a decade or more and are living content where God has them here and now, these are a few things to keep in mind:

- Live deliberately.
- Be reflective.
- Seek balance in life.

- View life as an adventure.
- Take reality in stride.
- Continue to hope for marriage (until God convicts you otherwise).
- Have an elastic view of the future.
- Have a sense of purpose anchored in God.
- Be sober about vulnerabilities and make choices accordingly.
- Be encouraged by what God has done up to this point in your life.

Looking Forward

Journeying on foot takes endurance, and some terrains test us more than others. On a grade-school field trip to a beach on the east side of Lake Michigan, I learned that sand dunes are deceptively difficult to climb. The sand gives way under each step, so it requires about twice the effort as scaling a hill of firm ground.

A teacher who had grown up spending summers at the dunes gave us a strategy for conquering them. If you look too far ahead up the dune, he cautioned, you'll only get discouraged when the destination never seems to get any closer. Look down at the ground immediately in front of your feet, and concentrate on putting one foot in front of the other. Then take a rest every so often and look back to see the ground you've gained.

Life requires the same strategy: faithful perseverance to keep putting one foot in front of the other. For many of the women I interviewed, knowing they have fulfilled their responsibility to walk faithfully is a source of contentment. Perseverance yields a sense of satisfaction, and those women who seemed most comfortable with their singleness could look back with a sense of accomplishment after emerging from struggles in their past.

But some women expressed an even deeper sense of gratitude for what God has been doing while they've been trudging along. His perseverance in guiding and molding their lives has left them amazed. He has done things they had not expected or even wanted, but things they readily admit have been for their good and His glory:

- "I guess I'd like to be married and already have some kids, but then again, when I think about what I've done, there's nothing that I would have wanted to miss."
- "God has stretched me and grown me in ways that I could not have imagined."
- "I know that the Lord will direct my life to best honor Him, and if that means I'm single for the rest of my life, I'll praise Him for it."

The Israelites experienced this same work of God in their midst. The Old Testament tells of their setting up monuments of stones to testify to God's intervention on their behalf—where He parted the water, where He helped them prevail in battle, where He provided for their physical needs.

Tracing the outlines of God's work in your past makes it possible to look forward to God's grace in the future. What evidence do you have of God's grace along your path? Where have you seen Him protect you and provide for your spiritual, physical, and emotional needs? What can you praise Him for? Actively watch for God's hand in your life, and seek to discern the ways that He is answering the prayers of your heart.

If you cannot discern His hand at work, pray to be able to recognize it. Agitation of spirit is an indication that we need to actively engage God—to pursue, wrestle, cry out, and badger God until we are reconciled to Him and His purposes.

"What is to be done when the promises of God are denied by the facts of experience?" asked one preacher. "Turn the promises into prayers and plead them before God."

God has not promised that life will always be easy or pleasant. He has not promised to give us everything we want. Marriage, wealth, health, and the many other things we might want out of life are not entitlements.

What we can be sure of is that God is good and He loves us. Our circumstances are a part of God's working out His purposes for our eternal good. He has promised He will never leave us nor forsake us in the midst of all His work.

From time to time, God may lead us to that gracious plateau. From there we can look back in gratitude for the distance covered and, like the psalmist David, marvel at God's hand in our lives: "Who am I, O Sovereign LORD...that you have brought me this far?" (2 Samuel 7:18).

Corporate Responsibility: Notes to Parents, Church Leaders, and the Public-Policy Community

In the course of my interviews for this book, a number of women expressed the feeling that they had wandered into singleness without much guidance. "I was never taught how to equip myself for this unusual season of change in my life," said a woman in her midtwenties. "I have learned to make it on my own...nobody has ever talked to me about adult singleness. I have learned from friends and church and figured it out on my own. People need to talk about this phase in our lives more."

A twenty-three-year-old graduate of a Christian college said this: "You feel like a college freshman all over again after college—moving somewhere, starting all over, figuring out what your major and job really mean to you. We aren't given preparation for that." She noted a contrast between preparation given to young people headed toward marriage and those who are not. "I think church/family in general overlooks the necessities that living independently presents. Engaged couples go through premarital counseling to learn about finances, for example. You aren't given that foot up as a single."

Even some women in their thirties wished they could have had more guidance along the way. "My life has been so different from my parents' that it's hard for them to even begin to grasp my frame of reference so that they can give me advice. I miss that," said thirty-year-old Jen, who lives in New York, while her parents reside in a small town in Wisconsin.

Nancy in New York is the oldest in her family and thinks it would have been nice to have an older sibling to pave the way. "My parents do what they can. They listen, and they love me and want to help, but there's such a gap between their experience and mine."

Singleness requires community support, and so does the cultivation of a healthy outlook on marriage among singles. Researchers looking at the breakdown in the marriage culture in general are concerned that young people today do not have the proper knowledge base from which to build sound relationships and to understand the practical work that love requires. Graduating magna cum laude and making a professional success of one's life is no indication that a Gen X woman will be competent in relationships and love.

"For their failures and fumblings in this area, they are not entirely to blame. For we—their parents, teachers, and the larger society—have poorly prepared them to get themselves well married," write Leon and Amy Kass. "Strangely, even in the midst of all the current concern about 'family values' and the breakup of marriages, very little attention is being paid to what makes for marital success. Still less are we attending to the ways and mores of *entering* into marriage, that is, to wooing or courting." That's a call for parents, church leaders, community leaders, and policymakers to heed.

Parents

"My mother is desperate for me to get married," said Jane, tears suddenly springing to her eyes. We had been talking for more than an hour about everything from her siblings to her career success, and I hadn't expected to hit a nerve with this last question about marriage pressure from her parents.

"She thinks I'm a failure because I haven't found anyone. She is a sincere believer, but she doesn't seem to be able to apply that to my dating life." Jane, not yet thirty-five, has risen to the top level in her organization. It's out of character for her to cry in public, so she apologizes for the tears on her cheeks.

"Part of the reason is that she's not well," she explained. "I deeply want to be married, but I want to be married *soon* for my mother. I want her to know my husband."

Parental pressure can be one of the hardest parts of singleness for some. "For a thirty-five-year-old woman who's not married, parents can be her worst adversaries when it comes to singleness," quipped one Southern girl.

More than half of the respondents to my online survey said their parents had put pressure on them to marry. Even among those who are content about their singleness, it troubles some to disappoint their parents' hopes for them to marry and, typically, to bear them grandchildren.

Those whose parents did not put pressure on them expressed gratitude and said it helped their contentment. "My mom got married when she was thirty, after teaching in Europe for several years, so I wasn't raised to think about getting married right out of college. My parents do not pressure me at all, and I'm very grateful for that," said Rachel, forty-two.

The professional and social lives of many twenty- and thirty-somethings today are outside their parents' familiarity. When these differences create distance between the generations, both parties must make the effort to translate their experiences. It is unreasonable to expect someone to understand fully something they have never experienced, but precise communication and deliberate effort between children and parents can help bridge the gap.

That kind of communication can be very rewarding. Several women expressed appreciation for the way their relationships with their parents have grown during their single years. "We've had more time to get together and invest in each other, and I respect my parents more. They're in the same area as I am, so when my mom needs things, she'll often call me. Stuff like that helps me realize that it's not all about me, and my parents made a lot of sacrifices for me along the way," said Ann, thirty-four.

"I've gotten to know my parents' friends as an adult, and it's been kind of neat to see my parents through other people's eyes, and it's interesting to learn what your parents do but never communicate to you. I think sometimes when you're married, you don't have the same opportunities for lengthy, uninterrupted times together," said Lynn, thirty-seven. Taking full advantage of that time requires both daughters and parents to be intentional about building their relationship.

Church Leaders

"I wouldn't say my church prepared me for being single in today's society. It seemed expected that when you graduated from college, you got married. When I arrived home sans husband, it was almost as if they didn't know what to do with me. There weren't questions about my job, about my goals…it was always, 'So, are you dating anyone yet? What's wrong with these guys?' They asked with the most loving intentions, but it would have been nice to be asked about other things. Singleness is treated more as a ride on a moving walkway, rather than a stop in itself," said one twenty-five-year-old.

None of the women I interviewed said their church had taught about this time of singleness specifically. A few said that their church had prepared them generally for living as a Christian adult and that they felt adequately prepared as a result, but most women wished they'd had more preparation and teaching before entering this phase of life. Local congregations can give guidance to young people by encouraging them to plan well and to desire to glorify God whatever their station in life.

One woman mentioned a specific campus ministry retreat during her senior year of college that left her and her classmates sobered to the idea that not everything would be carefree in their twenties. It wasn't the message they had expected in the midst of senioritis. They would struggle and change jobs and have doubts, they were told. Now going on thirty, she is grateful for that teaching, which adjusted her expectations for the past decade of life and contributed considerably to her contentment through this time.

In the church, the division between singleness and marriage can amount to a cultural Continental Divide, that great watershed that runs along the Rocky Mountains. Teaching, programs, and the Christian community in general can be very couples- and family-focused, giving the impression that the state of marriage is the pinnacle of life to which all of us should aspire. But a wedding day is a false summit; the journey of sanctification will go well beyond it.

"I'm thirty-four now, and it's been hard for me to find my place in the church. At this age many of my friends are married and doing the kid thing. My church seems to ask, 'What do you do with these people?' They don't quite know, so they put you in this group…and it's been a strange age group," said a woman who attends a church in northern Virginia.

Being single-sensitive does not necessarily require launching more programs and groups defined by age or marital status; it can be accomplished through the intentional integration of singles into the body of the congregation as a whole. The activities of the church should place value on interaction across generations and stations in life. The body of Christ is made up of people from different situations interacting and sharing a common life.

The women who seemed more satisfied with their church's

approach were those in congregations that don't emphasize separa-
tion by marital status in the substance of their teaching or in the
structure of most of their programs.

A thirty-four-year-old in such a church said, "I appreciate the fact
that my church doesn't divide by singles. The teaching has holistic
application. As singles we should be learning from the role models of
married couples, and who knows how we might be an encouragement to married couples at certain times as well."

"The church I attend does a pretty good job of teaching that
you are here to be kingdom focused, and what does that means for
your life. It could mean marriage, it could mean being single," said
a woman in New York.

"I like how my church handles this. They've been very deliberate
about not separating out the singles, even though the congregation is
about 50 percent singles," said a woman who attends a church near
Washington DC.

Her church does have singles social activities outside of Sunday
worship. A number of women commented on wanting opportunities
to mingle with other singles in their church or in other churches, but
they also said that such events often end up feeling too contrived or
like meat markets.

"One of the drawbacks to singles groups is that you can get into a
rut of the same conversation over and over and over. That can happen
in any life phase, but the church is not intended to be this regimented
life-stage thing. It's about us as believers encouraging each other wherever we're at, whether we have cancer or we've lost a child, whether
we're going through a divorce, or we just lost a job," said Lynn.

The Public-Policy Significance
of Our Personal Experiences

While this book addresses the experiences of never-married Christian women, their lives play a part in a larger story of the social consequences of first marriage at a later age. Between 1970 and 2000, the proportion of never-married women between the ages of twenty and twenty-four doubled (from 36 percent to 73 percent), and the proportion of unmarried women ages thirty to thirty-four more than tripled (from 6 percent to 22 percent). For the age group thirty-five to forty-four, the percentage of never-married women grew from 5 percent to 13 percent between 1970 and 2000.

One consequence of later marriage is the potential for a declining birth rate. To sustain a stable population level, a nation's total fertility rate should be 2.1 births per woman of childbearing age. In the United States, the total fertility rate is currently just barely below the rate necessary to sustain the population. However, the current fertility rate in Japan, Russia, and European countries is far below the replacement level.

That makes the demographic situation in Europe, where birth rates are declining rapidly, far more dire than in the United States. Some commentators now use terms like *demographic suicide* to describe the situation there.

In Europe, the average age of first marriage is around 27, and the average age for a woman to have her first child is about 29, compared to 27 in 1975. Meanwhile, the fertility rate there is under 1.5.

If this trend continues, it will lead to dramatic changes in the European Union.

However, this population decline doesn't seem to reflect women's preferences: forty-year-old women surveyed in the United States and Europe in 2000 said that they had wanted to have more children. In fact, Europe would not be confronting the possibility of declining population if these women had given birth to as many children as they said they wanted to have, according to researcher Phillip Longman.

Greater educational attainment by women, increased premarital cohabitation, and economic pressures all contribute to driving up the age of first marriage and childbearing, say experts. "This correlation between secularism, individualism, and low fertility portends a vast change in modern societies," writes Longman, author of *The Empty Cradle: How Falling Birthrates Threaten World Prosperity and What to Do About It.* "In the USA, for example, nearly 20% of women born in the late 1950s are reaching the end of their reproductive lives without having children."

These changes have economic consequences for societies. Declining fertility translates into aging societies. This puts economic pressure on nations that depend on workers to generate support for tax-subsidized social security and health benefit programs for older individuals who have left the work force. As the proportion of the population that is working declines and the retired population expands, the strain increases. By contrast, population growth is generally recognized to fuel economic growth.

Changes in marriage and childbearing patterns also affect social connectedness. In a book called *Bowling Alone,* sociologist Robert Putnam documents the depletion in American community interaction and social networking: "Thin, single-stranded, surf-by interactions are gradually replacing dense, multistranded, well-exercised bonds. More of our social connectedness is one shot, special purpose, and self-oriented." Such conditions contribute to a vicious cycle: entering marriage becomes more difficult, and delayed marriage slows the "thick" social networking that takes place around marriage and family.

Marriage patterns—as well as divorce trends—have influenced not just the individuals directly involved but the culture at large. "Boomers [1946–1964] were slow to marry and quick to divorce. Both marriage and parenthood became choices, not obligations."

On their heels, we in Generation X are a "second generation of free agents," says Putnam:

[Generation X] came of age in an era that celebrated personal goods and private initiative over shared public concerns.... In both personal and national terms, this generation is shaped by uncertainty (especially given the slow-growth, inflation-prone 1970s and '80s), insecurity (for these are the children of the divorce explosion), and an absence of collective success stories—no victorious D-day and triumph over Hitler, no exhilarating, liberating marches on Washington and triumph over racism and war, indeed hardly any "great collective events" at all. For understandable reasons, this cohort is very inwardly focused.

Bowling Alone predates 9/11, and Americans experienced a burst of solidarity in its wake, but it does not appear to have turned the generational tide that is the subject of this book.

Putnam describes the unraveling of social connectedness generally as "a puzzle of some importance to the future of American democracy." The same could be said of the social consequences of extended singleness.

Introduction

2 "The average age of first marriage has climbed more than four years": *Estimated Median Age at First Marriage, by Sex: 1890 to the Present,* U.S. Census Bureau, 21 September 2006, www.census.gov/population/socdemo/hh-fam/ms2.pdf.

7 "unmarried women over the age of twenty responded": Neither this survey nor any of the focus groups or questionnaires are based on samples that would be representative of the U.S. population as a whole or the Christian subculture. The results of the survey, therefore, cannot be generalized beyond the 650 women who participated.

Chapter One

16 "the average age of first marriage for women was just under twenty-one." *Estimated Median Age at First Marriage, by Sex: 1890 to the Present,* U.S. Census Bureau, 21 September 2006, www.census.gov/population/socdemo/hh-fam/ms2.pdf.

16 "Nine out of ten high-school senior girls say that a good marriage and family life are important for their future": Diane Swanbrow, ed., "Family Values: Belief in Marriage and Family Life Remains Strong," *Social Science in the Public Interest* 2, no. 1, Fall 2002, www.isr.umich.edu/home/news/update/2002-11.pdf.

17   "Almost six out of ten women today are not married by age
      twenty-five. Three out of ten are not married by thirty":
      Calculations based on data from the *Current Population
      Survey,* U.S. Department of Labor, 2006, www.bls.gov/cps.
20   "In south central Iraq around Hillah": Coalition Provisional
      Authority, www.cpa-iraq.org.

Chapter Three

45   " 'The Girl Project' is what researcher Barbara Dafoe White-
      head calls it": For her discussion of the Girl Project, see
      Barbara Dafoe Whitehead, *Why There Are No Good Men
      Left: The Romantic Plight of the New Single Woman* (New
      York: Broadway, 2003), 77–97.
45   "Girls' participation in high-school sports increased nearly
      850 percent between 1971 and 2001": *Title IX at 30: Report
      Card on Gender Equity,* National Coalition for Women and
      Girls in Education, June 2002, 15.
46   "exploited two of the most powerful and unifying popular
      sentiments in American life—the love of sports and the love
      of the underdog competitor": Whitehead, *No Good Men,* 83.
47   "By 1982, women had outstripped men in the number of
      bachelor's degrees earned each year": U.S. Department
      of Education, National Center for Education Statistics,
      Earned Degrees Conferred; Projections of Education
      Statistics to 2011; Higher Education General Information
      Survey (HEGIS), "Degrees and Other Formal Awards
      Conferred" surveys; and Integrated Postsecondary Education

Data System, "Completions Survey" (IPEDS), August 2001, http://nces.ed.gov/programs/digest/d01/dt247.asp.

47   "In 1995, the proportion of women and men in the work-force who had bachelor's degrees was 23 percent and 20 percent, respectively": Lionel Tiger, *The Decline of Males* (New York: St. Martin's, 1999), 138.

47   "accomplished graduates of the Girl Project": Whitehead, *No Good Men,* 102.

50   "a strange discrepancy between the reality of our lives as women and the image to which we were trying to conform": Betty Friedan, *The Feminine Mystique* (New York: Norton, 1997), 9.

50   "makes certain concrete, finite, domestic aspects of feminine existence…into a religion, a pattern by which all women must now live or deny their femininity": Friedan, *Feminine Mystique,* 43.

50   "I am convinced there is something about the housewife state itself that is dangerous" and "comfortable concentration camp": Friedan, *Feminine Mystique,* 305, 307.

51   "repugnant" and "What is unreasonable and irritating is to assume that *all* one's tastes and preferences have to be conditioned by the class to which one belongs": Dorothy L. Sayers, *Are Women Human?* (Grand Rapids: Eerdmans, 1971), 19, 20.

51   "Are women really *not human,* that they should be expected to toddle along all in a flock like sheep?": Sayers, *Are Women Human,* 31.

51 "not as an inferior class and not, I beg and pray all feminists, as a superior class—not, in fact, as a class at all, except in a useful context. We are too much inclined these days to divide people into permanent categories": Sayers, *Are Women Human,* 33.

Chapter Four

57 "her hope chest is now her brain" and "credentials and skill carried around in [her] skull": Lionel Tiger, *The Decline of Males* (New York: St. Martin's, 1999), 138.

60 "Ambivalent About Ambition": For research and discussion on the subject of women and ambition see Anna Fels, *Necessary Dreams: The Vital Role of Ambition in Women's Changing Lives* (New York: Pantheon, 2004).

Chapter Five

75 "profoundly saddened" and "are in danger of missing out on one of life's greatest adventures and, through it, on many of life's deepest experiences, insights, and joys": Amy A. and Leon R. Kass, *Wing to Wing, Oar to Oar: Readings on Courting and Marrying* (Notre Dame, IN: University of Notre Dame, 2000), 1–2.

75 "Opportunity was knocking, the world and adulthood were beckoning…": Kass and Kass, *Wing to Wing,* 23–25.

78 "women are on the way to winning, but the conditions of victory may not be agreeable": Lionel Tiger, *The Decline of Males* (New York: St. Martin's, 1999), 8.

78   "Little did I realize that the sexual revolution would have the
     unexpected consequence…" and "The fewer the barriers,
     the more muddied the waters": Maureen Dowd, *Are Men
     Necessary? When Sexes Collide* (New York: Putnam, 2005), 8.

80   "Why, especially, when you called…": Jane Austen, *Pride and
     Prejudice* (New York: Dover, 1995), 256–57.

Chapter Six

84   "modern technology offers babies-on-demand": For more on
     the growing trend of women choosing single motherhood
     through sperm donations, see Jennifer Egan, "Looking for Mr.
     Good Sperm," *New York Times Magazine,* 19 March 2006, n.p.

85   "Because processes for mating and dating are not socially
     prescribed and not clear, women feel that they must make
     up their own rules as they go along": Norval Glenn and
     Elizabeth Marquardt, *Hooking Up, Hanging Out, and Hoping
     for Mr. Right: College Women on Dating and Mating Today,*
     Institute for American Values, 2001, 29, www.american
     values.org/Hooking_Up.pdf.

88   "A 2001 national survey of college women found that a
     woman usually had to ask the question or overhear the
     man defining the relationship": Glenn and Marquardt,
     Hooking Up, 38.

88   "that lacks broadly recognized social practices and norms that
     help them to place their present desires and experiences in
     the context of their future marriages": Glenn and Marquardt,
     Hooking Up, 65.

88 "Eight out of ten of the women surveyed said that marriage
    was an important life goal for them, and six in ten thought
    they would meet their future spouse before leaving college":
    Glenn and Marquardt, *Hooking Up*, 4.

Chapter Seven

94 "Companies like Perfectmatch.com and eHarmony.com hire
    psychologists and scientists to determine the essence of a good
    match": Lori Gottlieb, "How Do I Love Thee," *The Atlantic
    Monthly*, March 2006.

94 "Brief Encounters gives participants advice about how to have
    an enjoyable and successful evening meeting people": Brief
    Encounters USA; www.briefencountersusa.com/advice.asp.

Chapter Eight

103 "The Sense of Callings": This chapter on callings was shaped
    by teaching in *The Callings: The Gospel in the World*, by Paul
    Helm (Carlisle, PA: The Banner of Truth Trust, 1987); *The
    Call: Finding and Fulfilling the Central Purpose of Your Life*,
    by Os Guiness (Nashville: Word, 1998); and a sermon series
    entitled "Callings" by Rev. David F. Coffin Jr., at New Hope
    Presbyterian Church, Fairfax, Virginia, 2004, www.nhpca
    .com/sermons.html.

Chapter Nine

112 "God is most glorified in us when we are most satisfied
    in him": John Piper, "We Want You to Be a Christian

Hedonist!" Bethlehem Baptist Church, www.bbcmpls.org/aboutus/Hedonism.htm.

114 "One can take a job seriously precisely because one does not take it too seriously": William F. May, "The Physician's Covenant," *Working: Its Meaning and Its Limits,* ed. Gilbert C. Meilaender (Notre Dame, IN: University of Notre Dame, 2000), 178.

Chapter Ten

121 "To see one's whole life as a divine 'calling' is...the cement which holds together the various aspects of our lives, preventing them from splitting up into different, and dis-jointed, sealed compartments": Paul Helm, *The Callings: The Gospel in the World* (Carlisle, PA: The Banner of Truth Trust, 1987), 53.

123 "calling without a Caller": Os Guinness, *The Call: Finding and Fulfilling the Central Purpose of Your Life* (Nashville: Word, 1998), 42.

125 "We are not yet what we shall be, but we are growing toward it...": Martin Luther, "An Argument in Defense of All the Articles of Dr. Martin Luther Wrongly Condemned in the Roman Bull," in *The Works of Martin Luther* (Phila-delphia: Holman, 1930), quoted in www.godrules.net/library/luther/NEW1luther_c4.htm.

Chapter Eleven

130 "It may be conceivable to love one's fellow man at a distance, but it is almost never possible to love him at close quarters":

Fyodor Dostoevsky, *The Brothers Karamazov* (New York: Bantam, 1970), 285.

130 "If I profess with the loudest voice and clearest exposition every portion of the Word of God…": Martin Luther, "An Argument in Defense of All the Articles of Dr. Martin Luther Wrongly Condemned in the Roman Bull," in *The Works of Martin Luther* (Philadelphia: Holman, 1930), n.p.

134 "You'll love being who you were designed to be": Arthur F. Miller Jr., *Why You Can't Be Anything You Want to Be* (Grand Rapids: Zondervan, 1999), n.p.

Chapter Twelve

148 "Pursuing the Fullness of Truth, Beauty, and Goodness": The ideas and anecdotes in this section and the following section ("Cultivate a Sense of Appreciation") were prompted by talks given by David Gordon, professor of religion, Grove City College, at the Spring Conference of the Reformed Presbyterian Church of Bowie, Maryland, March 2002.

Chapter Fourteen

162 "Christ…is the hard, immovable, unshapable, intractable Reality that banks the sea of emotion into a river that has to flow this way and not that, deep and not shallow": John Piper, *Taste and See: Savoring the Supremacy of God in All of Life* (Colorado Springs, CO: Multnomah, 2005), 164.

Chapter Fifteen

172 "What is to be done when the promises of God are denied by the facts of experience? Turn the promises into prayers and plead them before God": D. Guthrie and J. A. Motyers, eds., "Psalm 89," *The New Bible Commentary: Revised* (Grand Rapids: Eerdmans, 1970).

Epilogue

174 "For their failures and fumblings in this area, they are not entirely to blame…": Amy A. and Leon R. Kass, *Wing to Wing, Oar to Oar: Readings on Courting and Marrying* (Notre Dame, IN: University of Notre Dame, 2000), 2.

180 "Between 1970 and 2000, the proportion of never-married women…": "America's Families and Living Arrangements," in *Current Population Reports,* U.S. Census Bureau, June 2001, 11; www.census.gov/prod/2001pubs/p20-537.pdf.

180 "In the United States, the total fertility rate is currently just barely below the rate necessary to sustain the population": "Fertility of American Women: June 2004," in *Current Population Reports,* U.S. Census Bureau, December 2005, 1.

180 "That makes the demographic situation in Europe, where birth rates are declining even more rapidly than in the United States, far more dire": "Chapter D: Fertility," in *Population Statistics 2004,* Eurostat.

180 "Some commentators now use terms like *demographic suicide* to describe the situation there": See, for example, George

Weigel, *The Cube and the Cathedral: Europe, America, and Politics Without God* (New York: Basic, 2005), 21.

180 "In Europe, the average age of first marriage is around 27, and the average age for a woman to have her first child is about 29, compared to 27 in 1975. Meanwhile, the fertility rate there is under 1.5": "Chapter D" and "Chapter G," in *Population Statistics 2004,* Eurostat.

180 "If this trend continues, it will lead to dramatic changes in the European Union": Pavel Kohout, "Where Have All the Children Gone?" *TCS Daily,* 27 January 2005, www.tcs daily.com/article.aspx?id=012705d.

181 "Europe would not be confronting the possibility of declining population if these women had given birth to as many children as they said they wanted to have": Phillip Longman, "The Global Baby Bust," *Foreign Affairs,* May/June 2004, 77.

181 "This correlation between secularism, individualism and low fertility portends a vast change in modern societies. In the USA, for example, nearly 20 percent of women born in the late 1950s are reaching the end of their reproductive lives without having children": Phillip Longman, "The Liberal Baby Bust," *USA Today,* 13 March 2006.

182 "Thin, single-stranded, surf-by interactions are gradually replacing dense, multistranded, well-exercised bonds. More of our social connectedness is one shot, special purpose, and self-oriented": Robert D. Putnam, *Bowling Alone: The Collapse and Revival of American Community* (New York: Simon & Schuster), 183–84.

182 "Boomers [1946–1964] were slow to marry and quick to divorce. Both marriage and parenthood became choices, not obligations": Putnam, *Bowling Alone,* 258.

182 "[Generation X] came of age in an era that celebrated personal goods and private initiative over shared public concerns…": Putnam, *Bowling Alone,* 259.

183 "a puzzle of some importance to the future of American democracy": Putnam, *Bowling Alone,* 184.

Acknowledgments

Writing a book on singleness has been anything but a solitary endeavor. Ruth Keehner has spurred me on to pursue this calling, and her advice and availability were tremendously helpful. Tim and Barbie Jones have embraced me in their family and shared their wisdom and grace during this project, as in so many other seasons. The women of the Reformed Presbyterian Church of Bowie, Maryland, gave me the opportunity to hone these thoughts; the support of the congregation and the teaching of Mike Coleman have been a great blessing. Deborah Vernetti, Dan Garcia, Bob Morrison, and Seth Leibsohn have been faithful friends and wise counselors throughout.

A number of people helped gather women's input, including Amy Fox, Linda Gehrs, and Jennifer Wotochek. Grace Smith Melton, Rachelle Richardson, Virginia Wing, Jessica Brien, Lauren Calco Hammond, Liz Weaver, Kelly Pippin, Shanea Watkins, and Esther Springer assisted in research. Charlie and Sue Staines, Joanna Harris, Pia de Solenni, Brian Pinney, Megan Swartz, and Vivian Saavedra critiqued the manuscript.

I am particularly grateful to Hilary, Emma, Carli, and the many other women who willingly shared their joys and struggles, along with the men who contributed their perspectives; they are unnamed here only out of respect for their privacy. I also gleaned insight from the teachings of David Gordon, Jerry Keehner, Chris

Garriott, and particularly David Coffin, whose series on callings shaped my thoughts on the subject.

My thanks to Chris Hudson and to the Multnomah team, especially Steffany Woolsey and Lisa Bowden, as well as to my colleagues at The Heritage Foundation: Rebecca Hagelin, Phil Truluck, Stuart Butler, and Genevieve Wood.

Finally, I am thankful for my parents, who cultivated in me contentment as well as a hope for marriage, and for my sister Susan, who, in addition to her direct contributions, has kept our household going during the project.